My Life Among the Spirits

My Life Among the Spirits

A Memoir

Oshada Jagodzinski

HAMILTON BOOKS
AN IMPRINT OF
ROWMAN & LITTLEFIELD
Lanham • Boulder • New York • London

Published by Hamilton Books
An imprint of The Rowman & Littlefield Publishing Group, Inc.
4501 Forbes Boulevard, Suite 200, Lanham, Maryland 20706
www.rowman.com

86-90 Paul Street, London EC2A 4NE, United Kingdom

British Library Cataloguing in Publication Information Available

Library of Congress Cataloging-in-Publication Data Available

ISBN 978-0-7618-7426-3 (paperback) | ISBN 978-0-7618-7427-0 (electronic)

♾️ The paper used in this publication meets the minimum requirements of American
National Standard for Information Sciences—Permanence of Paper for Printed Library
Materials, ANSI/NISO Z39.48-1992.

I offer this book to the Great Mystery,
my ancestors,
my beloved partner,
the wisdom holders of my spiritual lineage,
my devoted spirit guides,
and to all the teachers of my soul.
Thank you. I love you.

Contents

Foreword

Minister Colin Bates

Four years ago, Oshada came to me with an idea for a book. She'd had a dream in which the spirits encouraged her to tell her story, and theirs. Without hesitation, I said, "My darling, you have to. Humanity is in spiritual and emotional crises. The time has come for the spirit world to speak, and through who better than you?"

The needs of the world have never been greater to bring peace, love, and healing into the hearts of humankind. I truly think the realization of the soul, its journey, and how we are all interconnected through the power of life has such vast possibilities within the hearts of humanity. It brings us into a reality of the oneness of all life and the universe.

You see, we are eternal beings of light, and the power to communicate between the worlds is ancient. Through the power of the spirit, we begin to realize that everything we perceive of this world has its origins within the unseen world. The power of life itself is eternal. A great awakening to this reality is happening more and more. There are many being born into this world who are seeking to understand their journey of life, their place within the universe, and their relationship with the creative force.

We are on the precipice of great change. Many of us feel estranged from one another, from the natural world, and most certainly from the spirit side of life. We crave intimacy and wholeness, and we are being called to a life of service, compassion, and forgiveness. In *My Life Among the Spirits*, Oshada bridges the gap between material reality and spiritual realities. She shares her vulnerabilities and insights based on forty years of devotion to her spirit guides, her angels, and her search for a deeply meaningful life.

Over the years, Oshada and I have worked together as friends and colleagues. Her story and her voice are important. I admire her ceaseless dedication to personal growth and the spirit, whether it be in one-to-one readings, in service to the Spiritualist churches, in the séance room or on Pine Ridge reservation, all of which qualify her as a teacher and guide. She is greatly beloved of this world and the next. She is truly an ambassador of the spirit.

* * *

Colin Bates has been a minister with the Spiritualists' National Union for thirty years. He is a medium, tutor, and course organizer for the Author Findlay College for the Advancement of Spiritualism and Psychic Science. He was also a featured medium on the Netflix documentary series "Surviving Death."

Preface

As a child I was an avid reader, devouring any book I could get my hands on. I was also crazy mad for horses, so much so that my girlfriend and I would turn tables and chairs on their sides in my backyard, arrange them into a jumping course, and gallop over the pretend fences. Thus by age twelve, I had two big dreams: one was to write the Great American Novel, and the other was to ride for the United States Equestrian Team. Now, at seventy-three, I have written a true story of never-ending love between matter and spirit, and I was a spectator at an Olympic qualifying event where a magnificent stallion changed my life forever.

I was an odd child and never quite seemed to fit into my skin. In my heart, I always knew that there was more to life than the adults around me were letting on. I wanted answers to questions, big questions, which got me in trouble at school and in church. Eventually, I realized that I would have to figure out this great mystery called Life with the aid of an invisible world that I was learning to sense, hear, and see. Time and time again, a spirit teacher or guide would nudge me in the right direction, and I paid close attention to their promptings.

This book has been a long time in the making. There was so much living and learning I had to experience before the day that my spirit guides told me it was time to start writing our book. I hesitated at first. I had no idea how to write a book, despite many half-finished attempts. The spirits asked me if I could start at the beginning and write for two hours every day. They said that in four months, which happened to land on my birthday, I would have a manuscript. I agreed to their terms and did as asked. Four months later, I had a rambling first draft that I mistakenly believed was a finished book. But that was only the beginning. Over three years of rewrites and seven drafts later, I now have a published book.

I wrote *My Life Among the Spirits* out of love and gratitude for the spirit world. I have journeyed with these cherished companions for more than forty years, through New England Spiritualist churches, séance rooms in Sweden and Great Britain, Sami rituals in Norway, shamanic journeys in non-local time and space, three Native American reservations with Seneca lineage keeper Twylah Nitsch, the Cattaraugus Reservation, sacred Lakota ceremonies on the Rosebud, and with the Chipps medicine family on Pine Ridge. What I have learned on this journey could fill three lifetimes.

Come. Journey with me.

Acknowledgments

Every life that has touched mine is a part of this book, and I am forever grateful. I am grateful to my mother, who instilled a love of reading in me, and who fought with the local librarian when I was a child to issue me a young adult reading card instead of a juvenile one. Thank you, Dad, for teaching me to ride horses better than the boys could, and for your undying belief in me. Thank you, Jeanette Wayne, for your courage and constant encouragement. I am grateful for my friends and test readers Judith Chason, Debbie Hallow, and Beryl Notelovitz for their ceaseless support. Thank you, Colin Bates and your guiding influences, for stirring my soul and reminding me that being a medium isn't what I do, but who I am. Thank you, Sal Gencarelle and Helper's Mentoring Society, for creating an opportunity to come full circle, back home to my spiritual lineage. My sincere thanks also go to Stephanie Rogers and Story Jam Studio, who helped me hone my writing skills. Thank you to Jasmin Portez, for reading and editing an early draft. Thank you, Pat Cizewski, a talented writer, editor, and friend, for your tireless work on subsequent drafts. A heartfelt standing ovation to Caren Schnur Neile, my editor, who turned an overflowing, rambling manuscript into a published book—who helped make my dream a reality. Thank you to Brooke Bures of Hamilton Books, for taking a chance on me. Thank you to Woptura and the Chipps family for inviting me to live on your land and be a part of your ceremonies, and for welcoming me into your family. *Wopila Tate Win wauspemakhiye ki wakinye, Wopila tanka!*

Author's Note

This book is based on the author's experiences that reach back over forty years. All the events are true, based on memory and journal notes. Some minor names have been changed, and some experiences have been compressed. While dialogue maintains the tone of the original conversations, some of it has been re-created. The book is not drawn from other sources; any similarities to other works are not intentional. Finally, this is not a "how-to" book, nor is it an endorsement of specific practices or a substitution for medical advice, clinical diagnosis, or treatment. It is nothing more nor less than the author's story.

Prologue

One evening during my senior year of college, my dear friend Michael came to my apartment for dinner. When I opened the door, I took in the welcome sight of his slight build, wavy brown hair and ruddy complexion, as well as the spicy-sweet aroma of his cologne. We hugged, and he handed me his black leather jacket on his way to the living room couch.

I was laying the jacket on a chair, when all at once such an odd sensation came over me that I got goosebumps. I became acutely aware that the energy in the room had shifted, and I realized that I was sensing an otherworldly presence.

Not only that, but I knew who it was.

The ground didn't shake. The heavens didn't open. I didn't feel afraid, at least not really. I was a little nervous, but somehow, at the same time, a calm certainty flowed through me. It seemed like the most natural thing in the world to carry the message I was about to deliver. My only concern was how my friend would receive my words. I took a breath and dragged the orange beanbag chair in the corner closer to the couch. Then I sat down across from him. I must have had an odd expression on my face, because he looked at me expectantly.

"Michael," I began slowly, "I know this may sound strange, but your mother is here with us. She came to say good-bye."

Michael knew me well, but he could not have had any idea that this was coming. Our relationship, though close, was characterized mainly by dancing under glaring disco balls in the gay bars he frequented. What's more, we had never discussed his mother, other than the fact that she had passed some years before.

His dark eyes narrowed a bit. He swallowed. Then he said, "Go on."

I eased myself back, folding my legs under me. The unwieldiness of the chair was in sharp contrast to my sense of the rightness of the moment.

"She says, first of all, that all is well. You don't need to worry about her. But she also says she's here because you need to let her go. To move on. And most of all, to forgive yourself." I paused to give him a chance to respond, but he just sat there, his eyes never leaving my face.

"Here's what she's saying," I continued. "'The night I departed, I couldn't bear to leave you. You sat for hours, days, faithfully by my side. I just couldn't die in front of you. I couldn't bring myself to pull away from your hand. So I waited till you left the room to slip away.'"

Tears filled Michael's eyes and began to spill down his cheeks. By the time I'd gotten up and returned to hand him a tissue, he was ready to respond.

"I promised her," he murmured. "I swore I wouldn't leave her. But I had to stretch my legs! I went out to get a cup of coffee, that's all. I couldn't have been gone ten minutes. I've been blaming myself for years for not being there when she went."

We chatted a little more. Then the oven timer went off, and we both stood up. Over lasagna and wine, we talked about the surprise reading I'd just given him, and about our childhoods. We talked about other things, as well. Hours later, when we hugged again at the door, neither of us referred to our visitor. But we both knew that Michael had taken a giant step toward healing the grief and regret he'd carried for years.

I knew that I had taken a giant step, as well. I thought of my grandmother and her conversations with the deceased. I was stunned that I was doing the same thing that I had always dismissed or laughed at her for doing. It would be quite a while before I could accept and nurture this gift, but that night I began to understand the healing implications of speaking with loved ones who had crossed over to the spirit side of life.

Now, having worked as a medium for more than forty years, I often see clients devastated because they weren't able to fulfill the promise to be present when their loved one died. When these loved ones come through in a reading, the clients apologize for letting them down. The response from the loved ones is almost always the same. They say that they were being called to go to the other side, but the pull from this side of the veil was too strong. They didn't want to disappoint those they were leaving behind, to have them think they had given up fighting, to cause them unnecessary pain. So they waited until the person left the room, in order to slip away unhindered.

That night was only one of many mystifying experiences I've had over the years, some harder to accept than others. In the end, I believe that they all prepared me for the enormous upheaval, and enormous blessings, that were to take place in my life.

PART I

Learning to Listen

The world is a Divine celebration. The stars, the constellations and the cosmos have all come together to create a brilliant experience and test of life. You are an example, a perfect example, of that life. In you, each star has found a home. You are a microcosm of evolution. Each being, Divine in nature, is a creation of Divine light. Each one of you is Divinity. The hope of saving humanity from itself is to unlock each one's Divinity.

—My Lakota Spirit Guide

Chapter 1

Growing Up

It was my grandmother, Charlotte Jagodzinski, who most deeply shaped the person I am today. Grandma was of average height and, shall we say, generously built. She was a powerhouse with a single-minded determination to protect those she loved, especially me, her first grandchild.

From Grandma, I learned early on that there is another side of life called death, or continued life. My grandmother taught me that death had a lot more going on than most people thought. It was a world unto itself. You could still talk to people after they died. They could visit your room in the middle of the night and hold conversations with you, telling you things no one else knew.

In point of fact, my grandmother was a medium, although she did not refer to herself in that way. In a bit of a huff, she would have declared, "Don't be ridiculous, I just like to talk to Grandpa and my friends. I know they're dead. I can still talk to them if I want." Not only did my grandmother talk to her loved ones on the spirit side of life, they also spoke back to her.

Grandma simply didn't distinguish between what she heard in actual conversations and what she heard in spirit conversations. She knew which was which, but often ignored minor details like time and space, and life and death, blending the worlds to suit her needs. She trusted and acted upon advice from loved ones on the other side of life. Clearly, their opinions didn't count any less just because they were, well, dead. It made perfect sense to her that if her husband had reminded her where she'd put her keys or a sweater when he was alive, he would continue his assistance from the spirit side of life. Why wouldn't he?

Grandma spoke in clipped sentences and subdued tones during the "special" conversations, monologues, really, that she had with me. She always wanted to make sure that no one was eavesdropping, lest they question her sanity. Thus neither my parents nor my sister knew what was going on among my grandmother, myself, and those on the other side. They knew Grandma had special devotions and beliefs. But they left her alone, as long as she didn't try to draw them into conversations about the possibility of surviving death.

During our clandestine phone calls, Grandma would tell me stories of how Grandpa or her deceased brother-in-law came to her aid. She always spoke about what Grandpa or anyone with him was wearing. That's what I remember most fondly about our family in the spirit world: how they accommodated Grandma's need to see that they were well-dressed and clean-shaven in their visits. She was especially thrilled when they showed up in an article of clothing that she had given them. With every visit, she declared something to the effect of, "I *told* him that jacket looked good on him. He should have worn it more. It went to waste, but at least he's wearing it now." Love, after all, is in the details, and time and time again, Grandma's clan proved that they loved her by dressing up for her.

In short, my grandmother taught me that love continues after death. We are not alone in continuing to love our dead. They continue to love us back.

Early on, I didn't always take her word for things. When someone died, for instance, my grandmother always knew the deceased's last words. She once gave me a detailed account of a friend of a friend who was electrocuted in the bathtub. A radio, which had been perched on the edge of the tub, fell into the water and killed the poor woman, and my grandmother knew all about it.

Despite our history together, this story caused me to roll my eyes. It drove me crazy that she spoke about someone's passing as though she had been present.

"Grandma, how do you know that?" I asked.

She shrugged. "Somebody told me."

"But who?"

She never said. But eventually, I realized that she had been speaking directly to the woman in the casket. Once I understood, that became just one more dimension of our secret club.

Eventually, as the surviving member of our club, I became my grandmother in many regards. Spiritualism provided me with a simple set of principles that focus on spiritual evolution, personal responsibility, natural law, and the continued existence of life after the change called death. I officiate at wakes and funerals, saying meaningful last words to family and friends about the deceased's life. I counsel the bereaved and assure them that those who have died are still alive and love them very much. As an evidential medium, I stand before the living delivering messages from their deceased loved ones. For a long time, my communications always began with the person's cause of death, their deathbed scene, and their last words. That's right: the exact same things I used to laugh at my grandmother for.

When my grandmother died in 1995, at the age of ninety-four, I stood in the color guard line with the other women from the Polish Women's Alliance. I said a fitting tribute for my grandmother and sang a Lakota prayer on her behalf. The other ladies all said it was the most beautiful thing they had ever heard, and that Charlotte would be very happy with her send-off. Remembering Grandma's preoccupation with how my grandfather dressed when visiting her from spirit, I knew Grandma was delighted, because I was wearing the almond-colored suede skirt and matching jacket that she had bought for me.

As I say, in childhood, I knew to keep my mouth shut about these things. On the rare occasions that Grandma told one of her unusual stories to another adult, she would wink at me across the room. That was my signal to distract myself with something rather than jump in to her defense.

I liked sharing these secrets with my grandmother. It made me feel special. Equally important, here was someone who understood my sensitivities.

Although we didn't discuss it, my father's gifts were similar. One example of many occurred at the very end of his life. Dad lived a few months shy of his ninetieth birthday. He was bed-bound during those final weeks. Just days before Dad crossed over, his wife, Brenda, called me. She was concerned that Dad was hallucinating. She said he was having conversations with relatives who were in the spirit world. Brenda was surprised by the extent of the conversations and the stream of otherworldly visitors that kept Dad company.

What disturbed Brenda the most was that Dad kept talking about a nurse who was a nun. He repeatedly told his wife that this person was sitting by his bedside watching over him, and that he felt comforted by her presence. I assured Brenda that Dad was not delusional. The story that I had heard so many years before was occurring once again. Time and space meant nothing. This had been Dad's beloved caretaker from when he had peritonitis from a ruptured appendix and was battling for life at the age of twelve, and she was still with him. His nurse, who was also a nun, was by his side, prepared to comfort and assist him on his journey, just as she had done seventy-eight years before. Dad was seeing things, but most assuredly, he was not losing his mind. He was simply visiting with an old friend.

After Dad died, I heard from him several times. The first time, not long after his death, I was attending a mediumship demonstration with a group of about forty people. Dad was the first contact of the evening, which made perfect sense to me. In his earthly life, he brimmed with enthusiasm and was not known for waiting his turn. My father came through the medium with the same force and power he had had while on the earth plane. He was positively bursting with excitement.

In the message I received that night, Dad said he was grateful for the last months of his life, when we had become especially close. He appreciated my visits and the daily phone calls in the last seven weeks. He said he sent me home because he wanted me to get on with my life. The medium also referenced memories from my childhood that had brought us joy. My father acknowledged things that he wished he had done differently, and apologized for any pain he had caused me. Lastly, he told me how proud he was of me and that he loved me. I was happy and felt a sense of peace.

I could feel my father's presence surrounding me. He was a part of the conversation, and I was aware of his presence. As the evening's demonstration continued, Dad stayed, taking every opportunity to say one more thing just like he would have done in life. In every connection the medium made that night, he brought through a father. There were no other relationships, only fathers. One by one, people accepted their messages. However, in each message, there was always something just a little off. The message recipients were happy with their communication, but throughout the night, there were always one or two pieces of information that the sitters, those receiving messages, could not verify.

I sat quietly at the back of the room, listening to my father slipping in message after message to me in each of the contacts the medium made. Because it was the first time I'd heard from Dad since his crossing, I did not ask him to stop in order to allow others to communicate. I rarely get messages in public groups, but this time, I needed to hear through an outside source that my father was alive, albeit in another dimension, and happy. I sat in the last row with a huge grin on my face, taking in all the love my father was sending me.

As the evening drew to an end and the spirit power dwindled, the medium had one more message he wanted to give. There was another woman in the audience who was also wearing yellow. She had on a shiny yellow rain slicker. In his final effort, the medium singled her out and said that her father died at 7:17 p.m. The woman was like a deer in the headlights, because she could not accept that very specific information. In fact, my dad transitioned to spirit on July 17, that is, 7/17. Dad wanted to make sure that I knew he was right there with me.

In many ways, I was an odd child. I had my own sense of color and fashion that drove my mother crazy. Left to my own devices, I would combine plaids, paisleys, and prints in a single outfit. I also had allergies. My skin would erupt in rashes and eczema from consuming everything from cow's milk to string beans. Unfortunately, chocolate was smack dab in the middle of my forbidden foods.

Worst of all, I had borderline rheumatic fever, which meant that my physical activity was severely restricted, limiting my ability to be a free spirit and enjoy life. I didn't know how to fit in with others, because I was too busy trying to fit into my own skin. I always felt like I shouldn't be in a body at all.

It was clear to me that my experiences and insights were different from those of other children. I heard footsteps in my room at night. I felt temperature differences in the air that startled me. I often felt or saw a presence that

I did not understand. In reality, I was psychic. I could feel people's thoughts and emotions, knowing when they were suffering. Sometimes I would blurt out statements that surprised both me and others.

One day, I asked my mother why somebody we knew was so unhappy.

"What on earth are you talking about?" she asked, raising an eyebrow. "She's just fine. Leave her alone and go clean your room—and stop thinking so much!"

Instead of leaving the woman alone, however, I made it a point to spend time with her, trying to cheer her up with childish offerings like silly knock-knock jokes or a hug. I told her I loved her and asked her to play with me. We sat on her front stoop, and she told me a story. When I left her, I felt sure her mood had improved.

Years later, as I developed healing abilities and understood that the role of the shaman in a community is to bear witness to another's suffering, I realized simply being present, fully present with another, makes a difference. But as a child, I knew this intuitively. The people I spent time with seemed appreciative of my visits.

I grew up in an observant Catholic family and went to Catholic school for fourteen years. As a very young child, I believed in God with all my heart.

My best friend, Carol, lived two doors down from me. She was Lutheran and went to public school. Although my destination was a few blocks further down the road, we walked to and from school together.

Carol was the nicest of all my friends. She was gentle and a peacemaker. We spent hours riding our bikes, climbing trees, and playing board games. She never picked on any of the neighborhood kids. She never made fun of anyone or gossiped. She never put gum in their hair or called them names. We invented both winter and summer games that we played together. We even went on vacations with each other's families.

My first great questioning of my faith came when I was eight years old. I was distraught when I found out from a priest that Carol would not be eligible to go to heaven when she died. She had not been baptized in the one, holy Catholic and apostolic church. Unfortunately, Carol had been baptized in the Lutheran Church. So when she died, she would go to a place called Limbo, and not heaven. She would have to wait until the end of the world when Jesus would liberate all the souls in Limbo and personally take them to heaven.

A big reader and enthusiastic debater, I could not take this information quietly. I didn't understand how I would be eligible to go to heaven just because I was baptized in the proper church, but Carol wouldn't. Truth be told, Carol was a much nicer person than I. For that reason alone, it just didn't seem right.

"Why?" I asked. "Why can't Carol go to heaven when she dies? It's not fair! I don't want to go to heaven either if my friend can't go!"

Of course, no one could give me an explanation that made sense. The clear message I got was that I was not supposed to do my own thinking. All the thinking had already been done for me, long ago. My job was to accept other people's conclusions. I was told that faith means you accept things without knowing how it all works. This did not sit well with me. It created a serious rupture in my faith. I still believed in God. I just didn't believe in *their* God.

Little by little, I realized that there were too many rules in the Church that were not reasonable to me. I needed a more personal and expressive relationship with God and spirituality. If no one was going to give me the answers I needed, I would have to learn how to have my own conversations with God, His angels and spirit helpers directly. I needed something more meaningful that I could moor my heart to. Fortunately, I eventually anchored my heart directly to a spirituality that made sense to me.

As I got older, the world made less and less sense to me. I had a lot to figure out on my own. I was up to the task, but it would take time. It seemed that everyone around me, all the adults, were telling me that the emperor was wearing a beautiful set of robes. I kept looking. I tried to see things their way, but I couldn't. All I could see was a very proud, but naked emperor.

I was soon branded a troublemaker. An agitator. One of the nuns took me aside one day and asked, "Why can't you be nice like your little sister? She does what she's told."

Because I had trouble relating to other human beings, I preferred animals. They told the truth; they never had a hidden agenda. And, most importantly, they didn't expect me to be someone I wasn't. They saved me from the isolation I often felt while growing up.

My greatest refuge was at the local stables. It was easy to tell a horse all my troubles. There was nothing more comforting than burying my head in a horse's neck, breathing in its delicious smell, and holding on as tight as I could. I would cry into those strong shoulders and have my back nuzzled as I poured out my anxieties. There was magic and safety in those moments. I spent hours at the stable grooming horses, cleaning out their stalls, polishing their tack, and riding them. I lived and breathed only to go to the barn. Horses filled a need in me for intuition and compassion that the humans in my life either couldn't, or wouldn't. They understood my sensitivities because they had them, too. I saw how they pricked up their ears and used them like antennae to catch sounds and vibrations that were not yet evident to human sense. We both responded to vibrational energy, mere thoughts, things not quite apparent.

Given my interest in animals, I was delighted when my parents took me, at age ten, to see the new Disney film "101 Dalmatians" in our local theater in Chicago. We were seated together, popcorn boxes in hand, when for some reason I had an urge to turn and look at the back of the room. Behind the last row of seats stood a man leaning against the wall. Except it wasn't an ordinary man. I knew at once that it was a spirit man.

He was of medium height and build, perhaps a little taller than average. But he looked like a ghost in man's clothing. He wore a brown suit with a matching brown hat perched atop his white head. Mostly, his face looked like it was bandaged in white strips of cloth. But sometimes, it would simply dissolve into a pale mist.

At the time, my only frame of reference for ghosts was Casper the Friendly Ghost, so I was more curious than afraid. The ghost simply grabbed my attention. I kept turning around every few minutes to see if he was still there. I wondered who he was and why he had appeared. At some point, he left, and I could turn my full attention back to the screen. Later, my parents asked why I had been looking around. I knew enough not to explain.

The incident stood out in my mind because the man seemed so solid, and he stayed around for a while. Normally, I tried to ignore most of these occurrences because they were fleeting. I was able to compartmentalize what I saw and did my best to live an ordinary life, managing to convince myself that my eyes were playing tricks on me. If I rubbed them real hard, everything would come back into focus like it was supposed to.

By the time I entered my teens, I had pretty well persuaded myself that I hadn't seen what I'd seen. Although I blocked out many of these experiences, they had an impact on me. Deep down, I could not truly deny what had happened. I knew that all the people I saw were not the same. I knew some were more real than others.

It came as no surprise to anyone that when I turned seventeen, I left the Catholic Church. My mother insisted that it was because I was lazy and didn't want to get up on Sunday mornings. But I knew that my heart, and my faith, had long ago left the Church behind. Unfortunately, I was about to get lost in the undertow.

Chapter 2

College

I started college in 1968. I was derailed when I left home to go ninety miles away to Marquette University, a Jesuit institution in Milwaukee. I had gone to a small, all-girls Catholic high school, the Immaculata, on Irving Park Road and the lakefront in downtown Chicago. It was a safe, nurturing environment for me. One of the nuns, Sister Helen, took me under her wing.

Although I was rebelling against my faith, not searching for a faith when I went to Marquette, I'd lived inside the world of Catholic education for so long that it did not occur to me to go to a different type of college. The thought of leaving home intimidated me, and going to Marquette seemed like a safe choice.

From the beginning, I threw myself into journalism courses, with dreams of one day writing the great American novel. I planned to get my doctorate in world literature and teach at the college level. Thanks to the kind nun who encouraged me in high school, I already saw myself as a writer and a poet, destined for fabulous things.

At the time, college students across the country were majoring in free love, drugs, and alcohol. I knew plenty of people who sailed through college drunk and high. My popular roommate was particularly adept at handling the loud parties and other activities. But not me. I had no idea how to manage the overstimulation on a college campus. I found it almost impossible to sleep in my dorm room. All in all, it was a strange environment with too many energies washing over me.

Years later, while sitting in a meeting of Alcoholics Anonymous, I remember a beautiful strong woman said, "The addicts and alcoholics are the sensitives of the world." Thelma was a Native American woman whose face and hands were lined with creases and wisdom. She spoke with the deep kind of knowing that came from experience. She continued, "They wear their hearts on their sleeves, and they need to learn how to gently put their hearts back in their chests where they belong."

These simple words resonated in my heart. It was as though she were speaking directly to me. I was the girl who cried at Hallmark commercials, who could not bear the suffering in the world, and who did not understand man's inhumanity to man. I naively believed that life was supposed to be fair. At the time, I did not know that a medium is also called a "sensitive." That understanding would come later, when I joined a Spiritualist Church and started to unfold my mediumship abilities. I learned that being a sensitive wasn't a hindrance, but rather a gift. It would be a relief to know that there was a place for me in the world, that there was a place where I could put my sensitivity to good use.

So there I was, just an hour and a half from home, yet completely lost. Confused and overwhelmed, I too began drinking and using drugs. Liquor, marijuana, and amphetamines eased the path into this new life, helping me cope with the unfamiliar environment, as well as the pressure of expectations, both academic and social. While drunk and high, I still didn't see any clothes on the emperor, but at least it was easier to pretend that I did.

My drug of choice was amphetamines. A girl in my dorm had access to super-sized containers of speed, because her brother was a doctor. Popping pills from this never-ending supply, I had lots of energy. My mind raced with what I took to be brilliant flashes of insight, helping me, I believed, to overcome my existential crisis and find a reality that would make sense to me, while at the same time helping me to withdraw from the tumult of college life.

I chased the pills with alcohol, having no idea of the damage I was doing to myself. All I knew was that being high provided me with a measure of relief. It numbed my sensitivities. It also gutted my dreams.

Unfortunately, like any addict, I didn't have a turn-off valve. There were never enough drugs or alcohol to quench my insatiable desire, but it was more than that. I was trying to obliterate my spiritual and emotional sensitivities, yet here I was, an explosion of feelings. I felt the pain and the futility of the world, of the Vietnam war, of family, friends, and strangers. I had no idea how to manage it all.

I slept less and less, and lost more of myself with each pill I swallowed and bottle of booze I drank. I knew I was living in hell, but I had no idea how I had gotten there, and even less understanding of how to get out. Every time I thought I'd found the answers I was looking for, I slid back into the quicksand I was trying to escape.

One bright Sunday afternoon in August during this time, I was driving into downtown Chicago on the Kennedy Expressway. As I approached an overpass, the light shifted, blurring my vision for a second or two. But I know what I saw. It was a black, old-fashioned London taxi cab, stalled right in front of me. Although the road was fairly empty, its enormous presence caused me to panic. I sensed the cars coming up on either side of me.

I had to make a decision, fast. Did I brake or hit the cab? I decided to slam on the brakes, which caused me to swerve into the next lane and skid to a halt. Time stopped. I felt like I was someplace unfamiliar, as though I had slipped out of ordinary reality. I looked around, still frantic. To my bewilderment, there was no London taxi in the underpass. Next to me, however, was a man in a light blue Chevy, also at a standstill.

In that momentary lull, we were the only two people around. I was shaken to the core. The man in the next lane opened his window, so I opened mine.

He said, "I saw it too," and sped away. Then, as though someone had pressed a start button, cars were whizzing by on either side of me. I stepped on the gas pedal and continued on my way.

If it hadn't been for the man in the Chevy, I would have thought I was crazy or that the whole experience had been nothing more than a trick of the light. Eventually, I would have convinced myself that I'd made up the whole thing. Regardless, the existence or non-existence, of a London taxi cab in a Chicago underpass was more than I was prepared to handle at the time. I filed that incident away in the back of my mind for another day, just like I had filed away the ghostly man in the brown suit standing in the back of the movie cinema years before. I couldn't handle my everyday reality, much less another plane of existence.

When I entered college, I had had a promising future ahead of me. This belief gave me license to indulge my tortured psyche, validating my troubling lifestyle. I was convinced that my problems stemmed from being misunderstood. But far from fulfilling my fabulous destiny, I flunked out of not just Marquette but also the University of Illinois, Northwestern University, and a few junior colleges. Somewhere along the way I also married my high school sweetheart. I finally managed to get an Associate's Degree from Parkland Junior College, then ended up at Illinois State University, with a degree in literature and a divorce. After that, I made a stab at master's work, but by then the drugs and alcohol owned my soul. The daily use of amphetamines for nearly nine years was destroying my physical health. My mental and emotional well-being were long gone. I was suffering from cold sweats, gripping intestinal pain, and heart palpitations. All I wanted was for someone to come rescue me.

Chapter 3

The Accident

On May 26, 1977, I was twenty-six years old and still scrambling to find myself. I was driving from Chicago, where my parents lived, back down to Illinois State University in Bloomington/Normal. I had just quit graduate school because I couldn't keep up. I could find no meaning or purpose to life, let alone academia. It was clear to me by then that I was not a scholar. I was no more than I an addict hanging onto the notion that I was a writer.

On this particular day, I was sober, driving downstate to an uncertain future, taking in failure with every breath. I was on the Dan Ryan Expressway with a stomach full of French fries and a thirty-two-ounce cup of root beer nestled between my knees. I was doing seventy.

Suddenly I heard and felt a huge collision. My hatchback had been hit from behind by a large van driving twenty miles per hour faster than I was. Upon impact, I tried turning my steering wheel, but quickly discovered that I had no control over my vehicle. My knees involuntarily gripped together, sending the plastic lid off the soda. The sticky liquid shot up and drenched me.

In the next instant, something happened that made the difference between life and death. It occurred so quickly I had no time to question it. I heard a voice. I didn't know where it was coming from. I didn't know if it was an actual voice I heard, or if it was the voice of clear knowing that came from somewhere deep inside of me. The voice told me that I had to let go—completely.

I intuitively understood that what was to come next was out of my hands, and that I had to listen. I had to trust. This was my first act of faith in a very long time.

Following the voice was not a conscious choice. My decision to heed what I heard came from a profound place of knowing. I did what I was told because I knew it was the only hope I had of surviving this horrific situation.

Instructed by the words I heard, I took my hands off the steering wheel and removed my feet from the pedals. I put my hands, palms up, in my lap.

I closed my eyes, relaxed, and then went limp. There was a crash, and I lost consciousness.

I awoke moments later to people standing around the car and peering in the windows. In my state of shock, I could make out a man towering over me with his hand held up to shade his eyes from the sun. I was strapped in by a seat belt that pressed painfully tight against my chest and stomach, making it difficult for me to catch my breath. My left arm was pinched between the car seat and the door. My elbow and arm were throbbing, and the rest of me was cold and wet, soaked from the soda. My head pounded with a dull ache.

I tried to grasp what was happening, going back and forth between the physical sensations that drew my attention and an awareness of my predicament. My brain and body seemed to be working independently of each other. I could not put everything together in a unified whole. It was as though a part of me had drifted off in the accident and still wasn't fully present.

As my eyes began to focus, I looked around. I could see that the traffic had come to a complete stop. My vehicle was on an angle perpendicular to the highway, slammed into a concrete abutment. Unable to move my left arm, I had trouble unbuckling the seat belt. I reached over with my right arm and tried to push open the car door with my hand, but it was jammed shut. In that moment, panic took over, and I started screaming for someone to get me out of the car. That was the moment I returned to my body.

Just then, a buzz moved through the small crowd that had gathered. I could see people shake their heads in amazement, the looks on their faces reflecting pure disbelief.

I heard someone say, "She's alive!"

Most of the onlookers were frozen in place, but two men sprang into action. They pulled on the door from the outside, but to no avail.

"Honey," one of them asked, "can you try rolling down the window?"

Somehow I managed to comply, and one of the men reached in and released the door handle from the inside. Then, with both men leveraging their weight by holding onto the inside of the door panel, they forced open the door.

"Seat belt," I managed to say. One of them reached in and unclasped the stuck belt.

I was floating in and out of consciousness. I could hear people talking, but their words didn't register. I kept trying to replay the other voice, the one I had heard moments earlier, during the crash. Those words—"Let go completely. Put your hands palms up in your lap and relax"—split the air I was breathing. I didn't know where the words came from, or why.

Meanwhile, the two men's concern for me was palpable. I looked into the eyes of the one closest to me and felt a calm wash over me.

"My name is Jack," he said. "You've been in an accident, but you're going to be just fine." He swallowed. "Does it feel to you like anything's broken?"

I managed to shake my head. "No," I said quietly. I lurched forward in an attempt to get out of the car.

"Just take it easy, honey, nice and slow," Jack cautioned. "There's no need to rush." He gave me his arm to help me up and out of the vehicle. "You were pinned in there against the door pretty bad. How's your arm?"

I looked down at the arm, which didn't quite feel as though it belonged to me. The skin was already turning purple, but neither the hand nor the arm itself appeared broken. It felt like a bad sprain that needed to be iced.

Comforted by Jack's presence, I stood outside the car, bewildered. My hatchback was crushed like an accordion; the rear end crumpled into what would have been the back seat. The only part of the car relatively untouched were the driver's and front passenger seat areas.

"Honey," Jack said, "I think your transmission cracked. You couldn't steer that thing. Someone up there," and here he looked up to the sky, "must love you. Grace is the only thing that saved you."

I waited on the side of the road with the small remaining group of helpers and onlookers. I was sticky, but unharmed. There was no blood or visible wounds, and I could speak. My eyesight was clear, although my head still felt a little woozy. I had been saved, spared, for some unknowable reason.

A police car arrived on the scene, and two officers approached to check on me and ask about the accident. A second police car arrived, and those officers spoke with the boys in the van. Several people told the police what they had witnessed. They all said that the boys had been speeding and weaving erratically through traffic. Two of the onlookers, now witnesses, said they saw them throwing beer cans out of the window moments before the accident. It was clear that the boys in the van had been reckless.

One policeman wanted to call an ambulance, but I refused, claiming that I didn't need one. I wanted to be with family and friends and not on my way to the hospital. Aside from my bruised arm and overall soreness, I insisted that I was fine. The policeman had me sit in the back of the cruiser while he filled out reports and called a wrecker.

When both officers were finished processing the scene, they offered me a ride to either the hospital or the nearest highway restaurant and rest stop. They dropped me off at a restaurant, where I phoned my friend Chester, who lived nearby. Chester picked me up and took me to his apartment, where I felt safe. Then he called my parents to tell them what had happened. It took my parents about an hour to get to Chester's place. In the meantime, Chester did what he could to take care of me. I lay down on his couch with ice packs on my arm and a soft blanket over my body. He brought me a cup of tea and stayed with me the entire time. He was worried about a concussion, so he kept me awake and talking.

After my parents arrived, Chester drove my dad to the salvage lot to see the car. Dad assumed that I had embellished the story of the accident, considering that I looked just fine, if a little shaken. But Chester told me later that when my father saw the car, he stopped dead in his tracks and turned pale.

"I had to give your dad my arm to steady him, because his knees buckled," he told me. "He wobbled, and I thought he was going to fall over." He shook his head. Your dad said, "My God! How the hell did she get out of there alive?"

When Dad and Chester returned to the apartment, my parents drove me to our local hospital. I remember being admitted to the emergency room. The doctor who examined me was kind and sensitive to the ordeal I had been through. When he looked at my stomach, he stood back and turned away for a moment.

The seat belt that kept me from flying through the windshield had cut into me. Welts surfaced, leaving purple ridges crisscrossing my chest and stomach. The doctor looked at me with concern and a deep sadness in his eyes. I was touched by his expression, and by the compassion in his voice. He asked me some fairly routine questions, and then he hesitated. He prefaced his final question by saying that he needed to ask me something.

After a few more moments, he asked, "You weren't pregnant, were you?" I remember he very deliberately phrased the question in the past tense. I could see the visible relief on his face when I said no.

"I'm glad to hear that," he said. "Because the bruising indicates that a pregnancy might not have survived an impact like the one you sustained."

After the physical examination, the doctor ordered X-rays. Thirty-nine, to be exact. He was stunned to find that I had no broken bones, hairline fractures, or organ damage.

Shaking his head in disbelief, he mumbled, "You are one lucky lady. Someone is watching out for you." My bruised body was turning deeper shades of red, blue and purple by the minute, but that was all. The doctor sent me home.

I stayed with Mom and Dad for over a week. I was too sore to move very much. Every time I tried to sit up or bend in any direction, I groaned from the pain. My body was banged up, and I was an assortment of mottled colors in various shades. More than anything, I needed to rest. In the meantime, I had plenty of time to think about what happened and what the future would look like when I left my parents' home.

For the first time in a long while, I prayed for guidance. I knew the life I was living needed to change. I was falling apart. I was lost, as lost as I could be, and I was too worn down to resist.

At the same time, I kept thinking about the voice I had heard. I had done as the voice told me, and I had miraculously survived. I understood that I had had no control over my vehicle. Events had been set in motion with the force of impact. I was simply in the center of the chaos that surrounded me. Instead of resisting, I let go of any attempt to handle the situation. I surrendered, putting my hands in my lap in an attitude of complete acceptance for whatever was to come. I had followed a command that completely interrupted the workings of my conscious brain. I chose to obey a powerful declaration, a voice so strong that my instinct to survive allowed me to trust it. And I firmly believed that I survived for that very reason.

The accident proved to be a giant reset for me. It was as though the spirits who had saved me were now guiding me and showing me a new path. I was being led by a gentle inner voice that caught my attention every time I needed help. Now, I felt the spirits move through me with every decision I made.

By the beginning of June, I returned to the college town I was living in. I started to get to know these new spirits who had intervened to save me. I started to understand that they were an answer to my prayers and the solution to my desperation. The spirits were nudging me forward step by step to find the life my soul was seeking.

The spirit influences weren't controlling me or my mind. I understood that the spirits, our guides and loved ones on the other side of life, respect our free will. For me, it was a gentle, even organic process. I asked for help, and help was made available. Thoughts and possibilities came to my mind. It was like a window had opened, and a soft, refreshing breeze washed over me.

When I was drinking and taking drugs I'd lost my connection to the Divine, to myself, to the power of my own soul. I was frozen. I could neither give nor receive love. I had gravitated to what felt good, shying away from what was distasteful or took too much effort. I was controlled by desire and raw emotion. Now, all I wanted was to have genuine feelings and for my frozen heart to thaw. I desperately wanted to be able to connect with others.

I started to rely more on my intuition and trust my natural instincts. By August, I'd sold or given away most of what I owned and prepared to move halfway across the country to Acton, Massachusetts. I was determined to pursue a longtime dream of training horses. Moreover, I felt a willingness to leave the past behind and embark on a new path.

At the time, I had a striking-looking quarter horse, mixed with some thoroughbred. He was a rich, dark bay with a black mane and tail. His name was Razzmatazz, Razz for short. Unfortunately, he had some resistance problems, not a particularly admirable quality in a jumper. Nonetheless, we got ready to move out East together.

By luck, or perhaps by cosmic intervention, I found a man who was trailering a load of horses from the East Coast to Colorado. Once he delivered the horses, he would be driving back east, passing through Illinois, with an empty trailer. On his return trip, he picked up my horse, as well as some furniture and personal belongings.

Razz went into one stall. My furniture went into another. It was an odd arrangement, but it worked for me. For three hundred dollars, I managed to move my horse and my belongings halfway across the country. I took it as a sign that the decision to upend my life and move to the Boston area was meant to be.

By September, I was settled into my new apartment, working with horses at a small training stable. The two of us misfits, Razz and I, found ourselves in some very exclusive horse country. Both of us were out of our element and were training hard to catch up.

The following month, there was a special horse show in Hamilton, Massachusetts. It was a pre-qualifying trial for Olympic hopefuls in the three-day event category. I had never been to such a prestigious gathering of horses and top-notch riders. I drove into the show grounds on the second day to watch the horses compete on the sprawling outdoor course.

On this day, the horses and riders tackle a large cross-country course. The imposing course spreads out over three-and-a-half miles of wooded terrain. There are thirty-four jumps over water, up the sides of hills, and off sheer banks. The fences, which can be as high and wide as four feet, are often taken at odd angles to trim seconds off the time it takes to complete the course. The horses are expected to finish in under eleven minutes, so shaving off a few seconds from your run time can make a big difference in terms of placing.

The hurdles on a cross-country course are solid and unforgiving. They are often constructed out of heavy logs and creosote telephone poles. If one of these equine teams hits a hurdle, both rider and horse may fall and seriously injure themselves.

I drove into the show grounds that day to watch the horses compete. I parked the car and gathered my sunglasses, canteen, binoculars and, of course, my mud boots. I joined the other spectators and walked the course looking for the fence I would position myself by to watch the horses, one by one, tackle that hurdle. Only a few horses are on the course at the same time. They start at timed intervals, so that horses and riders will not back up on each other.

Wandering off from the group, I found myself at a particular jump at the edge of the woods, watching every horse as it approached. I knew that each rider counted their mount's strides in order to anticipate exactly when their horse needed to leave the ground to clear the fence. Riders often made quick adjustments to their horse's pace and stride.

Familiar with the way the energy builds as horse and rider advance on an obstacle, I focused on each approach, counting strides. Anticipating when each horse would fly, I vicariously soared over the jumps with them.

I wasn't there very long when a rider on a striking chestnut colored horse galloped toward the hurdle where I stood. Clearly the horse had been working hard. His neck and shoulders were slathered with a white foam, and his nostrils flared. I could hear the thunder in his hooves as they tore up the ground. I felt the excitement and tension in the air. This team had my full attention.

As the big red horse advanced, I saw him strain against the friction of forward movement. I felt the power in his massive chest. The young woman on his back fought to collect him, to hold him back. She wanted to contain his power for the right moment, but he did not want to be checked.

The stallion's power built with each stride. I felt his determination and I took a step back, gauging he had two more tight strides before he sailed into the air. His ears perked forward as he calculated his flight. His focus sent a shiver down my spine, and out of respect, I took yet another step back.

At last the rider loosened the reins and gave the impressive chestnut his head. She might have been on his back, but she was only a passenger at this point. Then, midway over the fence, horse and rider separated. He dropped from beneath her and hit the ground. Hard. He lay there, immobile, the life still coursing through his muscles a few moments more. A quiver flashed over his taut flesh. Blood engorged the veins in his neck.

The rider lay sprawled on the ground, but she wasn't hurt. She got up, brushed herself off, and, in disgust threw her helmet to one side. She was apparently angry that she no longer had an Olympic contender to carry her to victory. After making sure the rider was okay, her groom quickly stripped the tack off her fallen mount. Then without so much as a backwards glance, the two of them strode away.

I was stunned. I stood alone with the red stallion for what seemed an eternity. All life, all courage and desire had drained from this intrepid steed. The white foam on his heaving chest turned to a glisten, and that too faded into the ground.

Time stopped in the presence of this horse's sudden death. Tears streamed down my cheeks and mixed with the spray of his sweat. I moved in closer to the spectacular animal and stroked his head, hoping I could bring him some small comfort. I spoke to him in a gentle voice, feeling his mighty spirit shake loose from his mortal flesh under the touch of my hand. His essence passed through my body as it left his. For that second it was a world of just us two as I stood vigil. Then, the moment passed, and he was gone.

Suddenly there was a hubbub of activity. Men came with ropes, which they tied above the red horse's hooves. They dragged him off the course into a clearing at the edge of the woods, so the other horses and riders could come through. Eventually, a truck came to take his body. I stood there with my new friend, respectfully, until he was ushered away. But the girl who rode him, the girl who pinned her dreams on him, the girl who felt her horse collapse and his glorious life drain away from underneath her—she never came back. Her actions tore a hole in my heart, as tears of disbelief still drenched my cheeks. Her relationship with this magnificent fallen beast had clearly been nothing more than a business transaction.

Compassion and love created a bond between Red and me, even as we stood in different worlds, spirit and matter. With his death, I understood that death and life are partners, intimate companions that continue to interact.

After the stallion was removed, I walked away. I returned to my car and drove home, alone and in silence. That day, I also walked away from the horse world. My heart could not survive the brutality of competition at this level. Peace surrounded my decision. The chestnut went his way, and I went mine. Soon after, someone wanted to buy my horse. I sold her Razz and all my riding equipment and never looked back.

The red stallion had suffered a massive heart attack as he sailed through the air, and my own heart flickered and changed that day as well. Both of our hearts gave out on the same battlefield. We both lost our resolve for the lives we had been living. This seemed like a moment of great purpose, a calling of sorts. Life and death intersected that day for a reason. Our spirits mingled on that crisp late September day in the fall of 1977, and we were both ready to move on to a more spiritual life. I never looked back or questioned my decision to meet my destiny. I had moved to Massachusetts for a reason, one that was slowly becoming apparent.

In retrospect, after years of shamanic training, I understood that I was being prepared to look at myself. There are those who can go through their entire earth journey without deep self-reflection. It isn't their path. It was, however, mine.

There are six directions: west, north, east, south, the above and the below, and there are animals that are associated with each of the directions. The horse carries you to the west gate. It gets no further. Once it comes to the opening, it throws you. When you fall, you are dismembered. Your psyche, your ego splits apart. You need to go deep inside and look at all the scary places, the monsters in your life, to be healed, to be put back together again. In these teachings, you must follow the wolf—the teacher—and then the bear, the one who hibernates, mimics death, but does not die. After you emerge from the teachings of the horse, wolf and bear, you have acknowledged a death, that is, the death of your attachment to who you thought you were. It is at that point that you begin to know who you truly are in the world. You find your rightful place.

This horse whose name I did not know—but dubbed Red—this horse who died a few yards from my feet, brought me to the precipice of a new life. It was this horse, a literal horse, that brought me to the west gate. A new life was waiting right around the corner, and I had no idea of what was to come.

More than forty years later, Red still finds me in the dreamtime. We journey and fly through time and space on healing missions for those I work with, or just for the sheer pleasure of it. He is always waiting for me to jump up on his bare back, grab a handful of his wild mane and ride. Sometimes we gallop across the plains with Phillip Chipps and Crazy Horse in the basin of Eagle Nest Butte—but that tale doesn't come for another ten years. In the meantime, I had work to do.

It was November, a few nights before my twenty-seventh birthday, and five weeks after Red had died. I was in my apartment, drowning in self-pity. I didn't know what was going on, but something wasn't right. Nine years before, I had taken the wrong fork in the path when I chose drugs and alcohol over life. Defeat and despair pointed the way, and I willingly followed. I mistook the feeling of temporary relief for hope. With each misstep, shackles latched onto my ankles, making it more difficult to change paths. I seemed destined to live not knowing I was the walking dead. I withdrew more and more into the shadows. There was no future.

I had no idea, not the slightest inkling, that drugs and alcohol were the problem in my life. In truth, at that time I had little self-awareness. I certainly did not grasp that those substances were making me sick and separating me from my capacity to love and be loved. I was clueless that they were the reason I was drowning in self-pity. I never suspected that my body and nervous system were tapped out from almost a decade of abusing myself with poison. I didn't know that my racing heart was due to amphetamine burnout.

That night, I lay on my couch, which faced the kitchen. The music was turned up loud; I was playing "Evergreen," with Barbara Streisand and Kris Kristofferson. This was my all-time favorite, feeling-sorry-for-myself song. Barbara was crooning about her unending love for Kris, and I started to sob. I begged some unseen force for help.

Gazing toward the kitchen, I suddenly had a moment akin to "A Christmas Carol," when Ebenezer Scrooge has a vision of Christmas past, present, and future. I looked just beyond where the carpet met the linoleum at the threshold. A yellow haze filled the room, and some sort of apparition appeared. After a few moments of disbelief, I saw that the ghost was me.

I saw myself standing behind an ironing board. My thoughts raced, wondering what on earth was going on. Although my vision was out of focus, I saw myself looking much older, at least forty years old, wearing a hideous, disheveled housedress.

All I could think was, "What the hell? That's not me!"

The vision was mesmerizing. My hair was long, gray, and stringy, and I looked haggard. When I looked closer, I spotted a tumbler of whisky next to me on the ironing board. It was straight up, no rocks.

At that point I felt my body shake out of control, and I broke into an icy sweat. I felt the deafening thump of each heartbeat. My head jolted back. My head and gut started to spin at the same time, and I stumbled to the sink and convulsed with dry heaves.

Seeing myself looking so worn and used up brought me to my knees in tears and desperation. I barely recognized the woman I was staring at, and yet I knew, from somewhere deep in my soul, that she existed in my future. At the time, I was in my late twenties. In a dozen years, I would be at the end of my road.

Then the vision got even stranger. Without warning, the worn-out phantom gathered strength and shouted, "Hey, this shit has got to stop! We need your future! We came here to live, not die!"

Terror washed over me. The woman, the future old me, continued, "It doesn't have to be this way. You can get clean and sober. You can learn the meaning of love, but first you have to learn how to love yourself. You say you cannot trust anybody, huh? That's because you're not trustworthy. You've got to clean up your act."

The specter of myself continued to loom in the kitchen. She didn't seem to be there to haunt me, but rather to serve as a warning. The spirits, including my own spirit, were showing me what I would become if I ignored the warning being offered.

White-knuckling my way through the night, I thought of the past and the traumas that had brought me to that point. I also felt the wounds of the present moment pulling me into the abyss, and the shame of failure threatened to smother me. I felt like I was trapped in a sticky cocoon that, with the help of my higher self and my beloved spirit guides, was about to unravel.

I knew now what was happening. I'd prayed for help, and it had come. My own soul, perhaps my higher self, was speaking directly to me. That night, I wrestled with the insidious pull of my addiction, but I didn't take a drink or any pills. In the morning, I found a number in the paper for a local women's recovery group and called. Just like that, I conceded failure. I was at the end of a long row of disappointments, and my way of coping wasn't working. I was finally willing to make myself vulnerable and listen to what others who had been down this same road had to say.

Drugs and alcohol brought me to a crossroads. I hadn't taken any drugs in almost two months, but I was still drinking. It was becoming obvious that I couldn't handle alcohol, either, but I didn't think I was an alcoholic. Once again, I didn't even think I had a problem—not a serious problem. Hangovers were a problem. My nerves were a problem. The fact that most everyone irritated me was a problem. Mood swings and depressions were a problem. But in my mind, alcohol did not seem to be a problem.

Nevertheless, I decided that I would take a little break from drinking, or at least slow down. When I stopped taking the pills, I stopped having some of the physical symptoms that were starting to scare me. I no longer broke out into cold sweats. My heart didn't race and flip-flop anymore. As a matter of fact, without the amphetamine rush that I was used to, my heart stopped feeling like it was beating out of my chest and was going to explode.

Chapter 4

Healing

The number I called was for a consciousness-raising group at the home of a local woman named Linda. Linda was a drug counselor and herself an addict and alcoholic in recovery. She told me on the phone that she knew the need for women who were trying to stay sober and drug-free to have a special place of their own. At the time, recovery programs were often male-dominated. But, she said, women had different issues and needed their own space.

A consciousness-raising group for women? This was a novel idea for me. I had always thought of myself as independent. I didn't particularly think I needed to be liberated. But I quickly saw that something else was going on here. These women didn't drink or use drugs, and, they seemed happy. More than happy, they were comfortable in their own skin. They were at ease with themselves and with each other.

I, on the other hand, was always on high alert. I didn't trust people, and I was definitely not comfortable in my own skin. I had no idea what that even meant. Telling the truth wasn't my forte, either. Addicted to high drama and chaos, I used manipulation and sarcasm to manage relationships. Nevertheless, I was attracted to this group of women, because they had a peace and an inner strength that appealed to me. I wanted those things and decided to stick around and see where it would take me.

Linda's group was, quite literally, an answer to my prayers. It was as if sunlight pierced through the darkness that surrounded me. And each time I took a step forward, the sunlight cleared the path for me to take yet another step. Linda was a spiritual healer and very psychic, and I soon learned that she worked with others in that capacity. She was also smart. I mean genius-level smart. I could tell that right away.

Somehow, Linda could see into my future. She could see and read auras. She knew that I was trying to emerge from darkness into the light. Years later, she told me that she had seen a bright light with me, guiding me. She said that she saw a bright future for me; this was my soul's path. Actually, it was my *potential* future if I chose to do the work I needed to do. Meanwhile, in the present, I was a child, emotionally and spiritually.

Linda came to dinner a little more than a week after my last drunk and hangover. I had seen her in the group, of course, but I never really *saw* her until that evening. She wasn't what you'd call pretty, but she was certainly striking. She was older than I, eight years as it turned out, with a strong, sturdy body and ramrod straight posture—she walked like she was accustomed to wearing a crown—that made her appear taller than she actually was. Her salt-and-pepper hair was cut short, and she was dressed in what I came to know as her trademark, semi-theatrical style: a jewel-toned rayon blouse and scarf, jeans and boots, turquoise and silver jewelry. The jewelry set off the gray-green of her eyes. All in all, it was a look that spoke of her mixed Lakota heritage. But the most interesting part of her was her smile. I hadn't noticed before that it came easily, and often.

When she walked into the room, I caught the scent of patchouli and cigarettes. The first thing out of her mouth, even before she sat down, was that she hadn't wanted to come.

"You see, I don't really like you," she said, looking me squarely in the eyes. "I see through you, plain and simple. It's going to take a lot of work and soul reckoning to clear away the shit you're carrying, the pain and resistance. You're really going to have to apply yourself." She looked as though she were going to stand up and then thought better of it.

"You know," she continued, "there's no such thing as a free lunch. There's always a cost. Sometimes the cost is up front, but, other times it's hidden. Sometimes the price is fair, sometimes it's not. But don't ever believe there isn't a cost. You have to decide what you're willing to pay to get sober and clean. How much is it worth to you?"

I said, "But still you came."

She drew a pack of cigarettes from her bag and asked, wordlessly, if she could smoke. I nodded and reached for an ashtray. When she had lit her cigarette and inhaled deeply, she leaned back on the couch.

"You've got potential," she replied, "and this work is my calling. How hard you're willing to work is up to you.

Since Linda didn't drink, I didn't either. I was gratified, at least, that she loved the food. And she was delighted by my collection of R&B, soul and gospel music. Over dinner. she loosened up, laughing heartily several times. I was dazzled by her quick wit and intelligence.

Then, after we ate, she pulled out a deck of tarot cards to do a reading for me as a thank-you for the meal. Linda laid down card after card and told me the story of my life. I had no idea how she knew the things she knew. And it wasn't just the things she knew, but the healing presence that emanated from her. I was mesmerized by this woman's inner strength and gentle charisma. She seemed attuned with forces greater than herself.

That night, I learned firsthand what it meant to be a spiritual healer. I had had no previous experience with people who worked as channels, or conduits, for universal healing powers. Linda explained that there was a constant stream of life force energy available in the consciousness of the world. She told me that healing energies stream from the spiritual realms into ours, and that through a lifestyle of purification, and spiritual unfoldment, anyone could attune their vibration to these energies.

I listened to her in awe. Then she looked at me in a deep, soulful way that gave me gooseflesh. A chill moved through the room and embraced me for a moment.

"You can do this work too," she said, to my utter amazement. "But in order to do it, you need to stay sober and clean. You will have to excavate the pain you carry around inside of you, expose it to the light of day. You will have all the help you need as long as you follow the sun. Remember to dance in the light of the sun."

As she spoke, it was as though her words landed on my forehead and entered directly into my third eye. I could barely grasp what she was saying, but all at once I felt different, lighter somehow. I felt reborn into a new life filled with possibilities. I saw that she was right: it was all right there, waiting for me to explore at my own pace.

To my shock, my craving to drink was gone. I'd had a spiritual awakening and felt a freedom. My mental obsession was lifted. As soon as Linda left, I poured the bottle of wine I had opened for us down the sink. That night, January 9, 1978, became my sobriety date. I found my way into recovery and was told at my very first meeting that my primary purpose was to stay sober and help other alcoholics. I was delighted. I needed a purpose. The best part was that Linda was right by my side every step of the way, to explore this new world with me, first as my guide, and then, eventually, as my beloved life partner.

In recovery, I learned that I would have to chip away at old patterns of behavior. Lying, for example, had by that point become a way of life for me. I was so terrified that others would reject or hurt me. I didn't know how to ask for help or admit that I didn't know something. Because one of the principles in recovery is rigorous honesty, I was endlessly confronted with my withholding and failure to be honest.

In short, I had to know who I was before I could begin to love myself, and subsequently love others. The woman in that car crash had had a frozen heart. As Linda said, my job was to let the sun, the light of day, into my life, in order to shine a light into the rocks and crevices that I had covered in darkness for too long.

After I stopped taking amphetamines, my whole metabolism slowed down. I was frustrated not to have the drive I had come to rely on. Learning to manage my energy levels was my first hurdle after getting clean. I was not familiar with my own energy. That seems like an odd thing to say, but honestly, I didn't know who I was. I certainly did not understand how to regulate my energy or my emotions. Emotionally I was a seventeen-year-old kid living in the body of a twenty-seven-year-old woman. I was expected to know how to live as a responsible a grown-up, but I didn't. In many ways, I was just starting out in my adult life.

Now, I stepped across a threshold into the light in complete trust and faith. It wasn't so much a decision as it was an outpouring of grace from the universe, from a higher source. It wasn't anything I earned or deserved; it was a gift. Grace always is. The spiritual power that lifted me up out of my self-destructive life was unconditional love, compassion with no strings attached. It was mine to embrace or disregard.

Alcoholics and addicts can have many bottoms. We rarely know if we have had enough, or if this is our last bottom. We can always sink deeper. There is always another hell just below the hell we are already in. My life had become unmanageable. I'd felt powerless to create effective change. I was like a hamster on a wheel, going around and around in the same insanity, thinking that this time, some illusive "it" would be better.

At the time, I had no idea if I would have the grace and the willingness to follow through with my good intentions. In recovery, they speak about taking life one day at a time—and in a crisis perhaps an hour, or ever a minute at a time. I didn't think about the future or what living a sober and drug-free life would entail. I had no idea where it would take me. I could not begin to comprehend that my sobriety would introduce me to my true self.

And there was Linda, right by my side, to explore this new world with me every step of then way.

"Every sensitive brings herself, who she essentially is, to her work in service to the spirits," she told me. We are the template through which the spirit world works."

I learned later that as mediums, we are called channels, empty vessels, vehicles for communication. If mediums indulge in behaviors that are not good for them, it can create tension and real problems in their connections and work. Therefore, the medium strives to align herself with the light and the higher vibrational realms. Alcohol, one type of spirits, or the spirit of addiction, does not blend well with the spirits, our deceased loved ones and guides, who communicate with us mortals.

I should point out that not all mediums believe as I do. For me, mediumship is a spiritual experience that uplifts the souls of all involved. It can relieve us of the bondage of grief and suffering. For me, it is not an entertainment- or ego-based commodity. So my journey of purification is directly related to the process of the unfolding of my sensitivities and mediumistic abilities.

I trusted Linda as much as I was capable of trusting another person at that point. That's why it was so painful the day she took me to Hampton Beach, New Hampshire, about an hour from where we lived. It was an early spring day. The sun was shining, but it was the kind of day you hunched your shoulders to protect yourself from the bitter wind.

Linda had been particularly provoking on the drive up. She generously pointed out several of my character defects and failings. It really irked me, but I just sat there taking it all in, getting more resentful by the minute. I had no idea how to deal with my feelings in a direct way. I couldn't even identify my feelings: they were all mixed together like something that had been through a blender.

Finally, we arrived at the beach, and I could get out of the car and, I thought, away from the pain I was feeling. We were the only two people on the beach that frigid day. We walked a while, and Linda kept poking at me with endless chides. Finally, she asked me to go stand by the water's edge with my back to the sea. She stood uphill on a sand dune some fifty feet away, with her feet squared off hip-width apart, and firmly planted on the earth. She'd fixed her hands resolutely on her hips.

"Tell me that you're angry with me," she said.

I couldn't get the words out. I was steaming mad, but I couldn't actually say the words. I had a lifetime of practice holding in my anger and destroying myself with it.

"Come on," she goaded me, "stop being such a victim. Poor you, poor you, pour you a drink. Is that what you want? Do you want a drink?"

"No!" I managed to scream. "I just want you to leave me alone. Why are you doing this to me?"

"Oh honey," she said, a little more gently. "I'm not doing anything to you. "You're doing all of this to yourself."

"I am not! You are doing this to me! I've been good. I haven't had a drink in months. I haven't had so much as a toke either. Why are you being so mean?"

At this point, Linda laughed, but not an ordinary laugh, more like a jeer. "Mean? You think I'm being mean? You haven't seen anything, sister! I can't begin to touch how mean you've been to yourself all these wasted years. Being a good girl isn't going to cut it. I'm not your damn mother. I'm here to help you get better."

Cold tears streamed down my face, but I knew I wasn't going to get any sympathy from her. She couldn't care less that I was using my shirt sleeve to wipe my eyes, or that I blew my nose in my hand and rubbed it on my jeans. I was good and pissed, and I could not hold back the rage any longer.

I screamed—at least I think I screamed—"I'm pissed at you!"

Linda snorted. "You're pissed? Say it louder! Say it like you mean it!"

"I'm so damn mad at you! I trusted you, and you're just mean."

It took more prodding on her part, but I finally let go. I started screaming at the top of my lungs.

"I'm angry! I'm sick and tired of everyone pushing me around! You can't treat me like this! I'm so fucking angry!"

By now I was no longer aware of Linda. Pain surged through me. Failure and shame ripped through me as the sea pounded the shore with a ferocity I had not realized was there. The waves slapped the beach, and then I felt an invisible hand slap my back. I continued to spit out the venom I'd been turning against myself all these years.

"I'm sick and tired of being angry! I am pissed about being a damn victim! *I'm angry!*"

I heard the words reverberate in the wind. They lingered long enough for me to realize that the anger wasn't inside me any longer. I'd managed to spit it out. The sea and the wind and Linda had pulled it right out of me. It was gone. I was stunned. My knees grew weak, and I nearly collapsed with relief on the beach, sobbing at the incredible release I was feeling. For the first time in what seemed like forever, I felt free.

Linda walked closer and took my face in her hands. Looking me directly in the eyes, she said softly, "I'm proud of you. You are a warrior. What you did here today is fight for your recovery. You're going to be okay."

I fell into her arms and felt the warmth of her embrace. With her free hand, she brushed off the energy around me, as if she were scrubbing off years of cobwebs.

Then she laughed, reached into her pocket and handed me some tissues. "Blow your nose, honey. You're a mess."

We both started to laugh as I wiped my face. I looked up at her, completely exhausted.

"Thank you," I murmured. "I can't believe you did this for me. I was so angry with you, and you were just trying to help me."

I had never felt this depth of gratitude toward another human being. I'd never felt such a profound sense of love. This was the most honest day of my life.

From that day forward, I was never afraid of my feelings again. I no longer thought that my emotions would kill me if I acknowledged and expressed them. I finally understood that I was in charge of them, and not the other way around.

I spent the next year and a half learning who I was. I started to really look at different issues as they rose to the surface. There was no shutting down the well of feelings or the multitude of insights that bubbled up. I spent most of that time raw with emotion. One minute I would cry from the slightest side-way glance, the next I would be enraged by the slimmest perceived provocation. With every step I took, I moved a little farther away from the woman standing behind the ironing board with a glass of whisky next to her.

Little did I know that it would be my destiny to work with the spirits, or that I had already started my training. I didn't know that my work in recovery would become the foundation for my work with the spirits. I had to learn who I was in order to enter into a relationship with them. Every medium has a different process, and this was my path. Early on, I learned I could not mix my work with the spirits with alcoholic spirits. It was clear that the two kinds of spirits did not mix.

During the same period, I had another spiritual awakening. At least that's how I think of it. I'd grown up in Chicago, and I was raised on deli lunch meat, and boxes of steaks direct from the stockyards. I also loved sugar and dairy.

I suffered from debilitating digestive issues and was guided to see a chiropractor who happened to be a vegetarian. She gave free adjustments on her patients' animals to make amends for all the animals she had consumed in her lifetime. She quickly advised me to stop eating meat, dairy and sugar, because I had a precancerous condition in my colon. She didn't have to work hard to convince me. After a heavy meal filled with animal food, I would frequently double over in pain.

That summer, I happened to meet a woman who was macrobiotic. I had no idea what that even meant, but she was quick to explain it to me. Shortly thereafter, without any special training, I changed my diet. At first, this consisted of eating brown rice, tofu, and vegetables; mostly broccoli, because this was all I knew how to cook. I soaked it all in copious amount of tamari sauce.

Then, when autumn arrived, I found a macrobiotic counselor named Lino Stanchich. Lino gave me a food plan and advised me to take cooking classes at the Kushi Institute in nearby Brookline. Before I knew it, I was enrolled at the Kushi Institute as a Level 1 full-time student. Once again, I learned to look at the world with a completely different set of eyes. Food, both its preparation and consumption, became sacred. I began to see a relationship among my emotions, my spirit, my body, and the environment. I began to understand that I was quite literally what I ate, and I made conscious choices about how I was treating and healing my body after years of abusing it.

I had never seen this bigger picture, this relationship with life. I learned that food is more than physical sustenance; it is energy, and therefore, spiritual nourishment. I also learned about the philosophy behind macrobiotics. It wasn't just about eating brown rice. It has to do with creating "One Peaceful World" and ending world hunger. Just as the urges to drink and take drugs were gone, so was my urge for red meat, dairy and sugar. I began eating a healthy and balanced diet, and after a while, the pain I had been experiencing was gone.

As a result of changing my diet, I became even more sensitive to psychic impressions and energy healing. My spiritual channel started to open. The food I ate, the food I prepared with great care, the food over which I made "energy spirals" with my hands, the food that I expressed gratitude toward, was changing my life.

Aside from attending lectures about creating One Peaceful World and a solution to world hunger, we learned about physical and spiritual evolution. Along with cooking and philosophy classes, I studied shiatsu massage, facial diagnosis, and Asian astrology, known as Nine Star Ki. I began to understand more about energy; how you can see it, feel it, generate it, and move it. And I began to see relationships between the world outside of myself and the world inside: my body, mind and spirit.

In shiatsu massage, I learned about meridians in the human body. I had never considered that there were invisible pathways of energy that moved throughout the body, or that these meridians could be seen with the spiritual eye. Over time, I learned to close my eyes and look at someone's energetic body through my third eye, and ultimately to promote healing in this way.

With each new lesson, another astonishing new understanding of life and the world opened to me. I started to see the world as energy. I learned how energy is moved, increased and decreased by vibration. I began to understand that my decision to be sober and drug-free was a spiritual statement, as well as physical. To evolve spiritually, I had to put down the false gods that had controlled me for so many years. Now, I was developing a spiritual power that could be used by the spirits for the common good in the years to come. That is to say, my focus was gradually changing from what I could do to make life easier for myself, to thoughts of healing, compassion, and service for all humankind.

Chapter 5

Spirit

A friend from the Kushi Institute had been investigating Spiritualism and the paranormal. In the early fall of 1979, she heard there was a Spiritualist Church in nearby Swampscott, and she wanted to know if Linda and I would be interested in going with her. We looked at each other and shrugged. Why not?

The next Sunday, we attended one of the services at the church. It was a quaint, old-fashioned New England building half a mile from the ocean, with a beautiful, well-groomed garden out front. You could smell the sea air the minute you stepped out of your car. Maybe it was that, maybe something else altogether, but there seemed to be an inviting and peaceful energy emanating from the church. Being at the Swampscott Church of Spiritualism just felt right to both of us.

Having left Catholicism over a decade earlier, I had not been inside a church in a long time, and I honestly didn't know how I'd react. But I could see from the beginning that this service was different from any I had ever attended. It began with spiritual healing for the congregants and all those in need. Chairs were lined up in the aisles, and the pastor, Reverend Mary McGuire, asked the healers to come up and each stand behind one. More than a dozen men and women rose from the pews and stood behind a chair.

Then the congregation chanted one of the most simple and heartfelt prayers I have ever heard. It invoked a great unseen healing power in the universe. From that first hearing, it was etched on my soul.

After the prayer, Reverend Mary announced that the healing chairs were now open. People began to leave the pews and sit in these chairs. I watched in awe as each healer behind the chair gently rested their hands on the person's shoulders. Occasionally the healers moved their hands to the top of their "patient's" head, or lightly placed them over the temples, all while soothing organ music played in the background. The healers stayed with the people in the chairs for a few moments, then leaned down and murmured something to them. Then slowly, one by one, the people rose, returned to the pews, and others had a chance to sit down.

While all this was going on, we in the pews were supposed to sit with our eyes closed, although I must admit that I peeked, just to see what was happening. Even without leaving my seat, I too felt a form of healing. Not only did the music transport me to another place, one far removed from the concerns and struggles of daily life, but the pastor also led a guided meditation that carried us to a special garden, a garden in our own hearts. It was a tranquil place to connect with our own inner light.

Afterward, Reverend Mary read a list of names from her healing list. It was filled with the names of people who had requested long distance healing for themselves or their family, even pets. At the end of that list, she read out the names of those who had recently died. She asked us to send healing thoughts to these souls, so that they might make a peaceful transition from their earthly life to their new life.

I hadn't planned to sit in one of the healing chairs, because by then I was feeling quite well. But the pastor made it clear that we could sit in a chair and send out our thoughts to someone we knew who needed healing energy. I had someone in mind who was struggling with a health crisis, so I left the pew and sat in an empty chair.

The experience was very different from healing sessions I'd experienced before. I wasn't receiving a transfer of the healer's energy. Instead, I felt as though I were immersed in a sea of radiant light. I absorbed the healing much as a cup of hot water might be infused with tea. The flood of spiritual energy completely enveloped me. Although I kept my thoughts focused on my friend who was ill, I felt that I too was receiving healing.

When the healing was completed, the person behind the chair whispered a few words in my ear.

"Your friend will be fine," he said. "She's just going through a temporary setback."

How could this man have known what I was thinking? I was amazed, but at the same time I felt too peaceful to question anything.

Then, a student worker approached the pulpit. At first, she stood in silence, eyes closed. Momentarily, the young woman began to speak the inspirational words that came to her during the pause. I looked over at Linda, and she nodded. I knew that she too was thinking it seemed like a risky business.

Next a male student approached the pulpit. After closing his eyes for a moment of silence, he looked to the left side of the church.

"I'd like to speak to the woman with the purple blouse in the back, if that's all right?" he asked.

In a clear voice she called out, "Yes."

"I have a gentleman here with me who is your father," he said. "I believe he's recently passed."

"Yes."

After giving a couple of details of her father's life, the young man gave a brief message from him. The woman nodded and looked as though she understood.

I didn't know which impressed me more, that the students could stand up and speak so beautifully with nothing prepared, or that they could tap into an energy field that allowed them to deliver relevant messages from the dead to strangers. All I knew for sure was that I needed to learn how they did that.

After the congregation sang another hymn, Reverend Mary stood up to speak. Again, she had no prepared notes. She too closed her eyes and paused a moment. When at last she spoke, the spiritual power that moved through her was more moving to me than her words, which I actually don't recall. What I do remember is that as I listened, I felt goosebumps.

The cadence in her voice changed, as did the tone. It became softer and more powerful at the same time. I didn't just hear the words she was saying; I felt them. The spiritual truths she discussed came alive for me. When she spoke about compassion, my mind didn't grab hold to the thought of being more compassionate. My heart was flooded with compassion. I was a part of the experience of compassion.

At that very moment I was sold on Spiritualism, and I wanted this woman to be my teacher.

Then there was the message portion of the service. After taking a moment to connect with some unfathomable energy source, Reverend Mary began to give messages in rapid succession. She gave a message to a lady with the red hat, a gentleman with the blue sweater, and so on. In half an hour, she spoke to at least ten different people about their loved ones. In every case the recipient said yes, yes, and nodded to affirm what was being said.

And then, just as suddenly as the medium began, she finished. The door to the spirit world that had been wide open a few minutes before was now temporarily sealed shut. Reverend Mary was once again an ordinary person. We sang one more hymn, and the service ended.

Thus Linda's and my new life began.

We immediately joined the Swampscott Church of Spiritualism and took an introductory class on Spiritualism and mediumship. For eight weeks, we learned about the history of Spiritualism and spent time unfolding our relationship with our guides. After that, the group was divided between one of two teachers, who held weekly unfoldment circles. To our delight, Linda and I were in Reverend Mary's class.

Once a week, about twenty of us sat in a circle, in the presence of the spirit world. Rarely did anyone miss a week. We learned that development wasn't something you did when the spirit moved you. It was something you did so that the spirits *could* move you and work through you. The spirit guides never missed a week, we were told, and so we shouldn't, either.

This was different than meditation. We were instructed to become aware of our guides and blend with their essence, extending our auric field and reaching out to the higher vibrational world. That interchange of energy allowed our souls to open, or unfold, like petals on a flower. Once my soul opened to the light of the spirit world, my guides and spirit loved ones were able to work to develop my spiritual and mediumistic gifts. The most important thing I learned in that circle was how to establish and maintain a strong connection to the spirit world.

In the beginning I didn't understand that I was working under the power of my teacher's established guides, her "band." They were lending me a little extra power when I sat in her circle. I also learned that sitting in a weekly unfoldment class was essential for the spirits, my guides, to develop my endurance. When connecting with the spirit world, I raise my vibration. I am in a rarefied spiritual atmosphere. As a student, I needed to build up my capacity to stay in that atmosphere.

One day after I'd been doing the circle for a while, Reverend Mary stopped me in the hallway.

"You know," she said, after greeting me warmly, "you're ready to be one of the student workers in the service."

She might as well have told me I was ready to rule the world.

"But—how long do I speak?" It was the only thing I could think of to say.

"Five minutes should do it."

Now I was going to be that person speaking in front of the entire congregation without notes, trusting my spiritual influences to provide me with the words I needed.

I shook my head. "I don't know. I really don't know if I can do it."

"Look, I know your abilities," she said. "You're ready. You've just got to trust that the spirits won't let you down. As long as you show up, they will too. It's just like when you show up in class for them week after week."

When she turned to continue down the hall, I touched her arm, not yet ready to let her go.

"Is there anything else I should know? Before I do it? Do you have any advice?"

She thought a moment. "Yes. Whatever you do, the lecture must come from the spirits. On no account should you interfere. And whatever you do, don't prepare comments as a backup plan. Just listen, say what you're told, and all will go just fine."

And soon it was I who was standing at that lectern. I too stood silent with eyes closed, emptying my mind and linking it with my guides. I forbade myself to panic. And sure enough, I heard a word. I opened my mouth and said that one word. Then came another, and another, and then whole sentences came spilling out of me. Before I knew it, my five minutes were up.

First I turned to Reverend Mary. She beamed at me the enormous pride and happiness I felt. Then I looked at Linda, and saw her gray-green eyes dancing with joy.

I had taken my first steps in this new world, and I had done well. If I had prepared some thoughts, or worse yet brought notes with me, I would have never learned how to open the door to the spirit world. I would have never understood the power of surrender that leads to a connection with my guides, nor experienced the blending of minds and thoughts on both sides of the veil, working in harmony together. My job was and is simply to show up. To this day, I show up and let the spirits speak from their heart, through my heart, to the people who are present in that moment. Each time I serve the spirits as their medium, it is like jumping off a cliff and soaring upwards. I trust that the spirits will catch me and bring me safely back to earth. I trust them as completely as I can. They have never once let me down.

Chapter 6

The Medium

In October, 1980, the church invited a guest medium from England to lead some services. Her name was Queenie Nixon, and she was a transfiguration medium. She would also be doing several nights of demonstrations at Sanders Theatre Memorial Hall at Harvard. Because it would be a large venue, ushers were needed for every event.

Linda and I volunteered for each night. We didn't want to miss a thing. We were both eager for every opportunity to learn a little more about mediumship. This was our first opportunity to witness transfiguration mediumship.

Transfiguration mediumship is, simply put, when a medium's face changes shape to resemble that of your loved one, the communicating spirit. It is as if an energetic white mask, a blank canvas, were to form over the face of the medium. The mask is fluid, pliable and can be shaped like clay to create a facsimile of your loved one in spirit.

On the second night of the demonstrations, Linda and I seated the crowd, then found our own seats. Queenie Nixon sat next to a table at the front of the hall. The lights were low, but it wasn't completely dark. Red "Exit" signs were over all the doors, and red lights were angled at the medium's face, making it easier for us to see the transfiguration.

It happened to be the first anniversary of the death of Linda's adoptive mother, and she really wanted to see and hear from her. Like Michael, Linda had promised her mom that she would be there with her when she drew her last breath. Although Elaine had been sick for a while, her death was unexpected, and Linda was not present. She felt that she had broken her promise and wanted to apologize.

Queenie Nixon deepened into a trance state, and her guide, sort of the emcee for the evening, began to speak through her. A male voice emanated from her lips.

"I will determine who the spirits wish to speak to," the voice explained. "I will find the recipient, or the sitter, through a series of statements or questions. Anyone who can respond in the affirmative will stand. Then, if you do not agree with the next statement or question, you simply sit down. In that way, everyone but the correct person will be quickly eliminated. Then, dear recipient, you can feel free to engage in conversation with your loved one when you get your molding, that is, the visual appearance of your loved one on the medium's face."

It sounded simple, but it was anything but. One or two people received moldings and a message from their loved ones on the spirit side of life. They had the opportunity to speak with family or friends and actually have an interactive dialogue. It was completely astounding to witness. Each person was overcome with tears of joy and gratitude.

After the last molding was smoothed over, the spirit said, "I am looking for someone who was born north of here." Nearly a third of the audience stood up, including Linda.

"You lived across the street from a church with a lake." With that statement, all but three people sat down. Linda remained standing.

"Your neighbor's name was Billy." Now, the only one left standing was Linda. He asked her if she was ready for her molding.

She turned a shade or two paler. "Yes."

With that emerged the face of a young woman in her twenties, with soft brown hair styled in loose waves at her neck. I didn't recognize the woman, but Linda said in a startled voice, "It's Mama when she was a young girl!"

As soon as she recognized the face, the molding on Queenie's face started to change. It was the same woman, Linda's adoptive mom, at different stages of her life. Each time the molding changed, she was a little bit older.

The spirit handlers moved the medium's head from side to side so you could see Elaine from the side as well as from the front. Then the medium's right arm and hand were moved to Elaine's face, and she kissed the tips of the fingers—and then moved the hand away and blew a kiss to Linda.

I knew that this was a gesture Linda's mother had done all her life.

Linda was speechless, but I knew she wouldn't want to miss the opportunity to speak. I nudged her.

"Say what you need to say to her!" I urged, in a low whisper. "Now's your chance."

She nodded. "I'm so sorry, Mom. I wasn't there when you passed. I feel so terrible about breaking my promise."

In Elaine's own voice, the medium said, "Don't worry dear. I wasn't there when you were born, either."

I alone knew that Elaine had adopted Linda when she was ten months old, nursing her back from neglect and poor health. That one, simple statement, proved beyond any doubt that the communication was genuine.

To my mind, the statement that Elaine made did more than convey a personal message of healing to her daughter. Elaine said that she wasn't there when Linda was born *either*. I have often thought about what she meant by "either." To me, it was clear that Elaine considered her death a kind of birth. The day she left the earth plane, she was born into the spirit side of life.

Elaine saw no difference between her birth into the spirit world and Linda's birth in the physical world.

I continued to sit in my unfoldment circle and to grow as a medium, working regularly on the platform and doing readings at fund-raisers for the church. In this way, I honed both my speaking abilities and message work. I was slowly able to build trust and confidence not only with the spirit communicators who worked through me, but also with my human guides and teachers.

That winter, Linda and I joined the International Spiritualist Federation, or ISF. Once a year, members and mediums gathered for a week-long conference at a different location around the world. We learned that in the early summer of 1984, the annual event was to be held in Sweden.

Although we didn't think we could afford the trip, we were amazed to find the funds at the last minute. So, along with three other people from the church, we flew to Sweden and made our way to the Southern Agricultural College where the conference was taking place.

We were sitting with some conference-goers that first morning, trading names and stories. At one point, Linda said, "You know, we almost didn't make it here. I won our church raffle. But that's nothing," she said, turning to me. Our new companions eyed me expectantly.

"Well," I said, "I was suddenly repaid a loan—with interest! That covered the airfare!"

"The same thing happened to me!" a tall woman said. She took a sip of her drink. "It was like once I made a commitment to be here, the money started to trickle in. I suddenly had a big boost in the number of sittings I was doing. And I just talked to someone else who was overpaid for readings."

The man next to her nodded. "I've talked to people who found money and others who received gifts out of the blue. It's as though we were all meant to be here." Everyone around the table agreed. And the more mediums we met and information we gathered, the more convinced we were that it was true.

At the time, Eileen Roberts was the president of the ISF. Eileen began the first afternoon course with what she called an experiment. She chose five mediums to work with, including Linda and me, a well-known British medium named Robin Stevens, and two others. As the youngest and least experienced, I definitely felt out of my league.

"I want you to trust me," she said. "That's all you need to do. I'm going to commence a spirit contact, and your job is simply to link in with the contact I establish. One at a time, you will each add a couple of pieces of evidence to the message I initiate. Just focus on the link, and you'll have no trouble conveying the information. Got it?"

The five of us nodded, confident that Eileen knew what she was doing.

"Okay, now I want you to go out into the hallway and shut the door."

I exchanged glances with Linda. She shrugged and shook her head. Neither of us had seen that coming. We exited the auditorium and waited a few minutes. Then the door opened, and someone invited one of us in. After a while, another medium was called, and then another. I began to take deep breaths and tell myself, over and over, to simply link with Eileen's communicator.

At last it was my turn to enter the room. I continued to breathe deeply in an attempt to calm myself. The last thing I wanted was to look foolish.

To my relief, I soon linked with the communicating spirit. I established that this was the recipient's grandfather, and he told me the age at which he died, as well as the cause of his passing. He also spoke about his illness and the family around him at the time.

At the end, after the last medium in the group gave the final piece of the message, the recipient stood up and confirmed everything that each of us said. I was astounded. And, when a couple of nights later I was invited to demonstrate on the platform with mediums from different countries, I realized that Eileen had a lot more faith in me than I did.

That conference changed the course of my mediumship. Every time I took a risk to open a new door, I was welcomed. Teachers and seasoned, developed mediums were happy to share their knowledge with me. More importantly, I thrived on experiencing the presence of their wise and kind guides. I was finally coming to understand just how real the spirit world is.

Toward the end of our stay, a professional photographer asked everyone to go outside on the lawn for a group photo. Some of us sat in chairs in the front row; the rest of us he arranged in rows according to height. Then he took several shots.

To our surprise, the photographer had to return a second day. He explained that in each of the photos, he had found wisps of white light, smears of blurry energy, and actual deceased people standing in the back row or sitting in the front. After that, several of the mediums asked the spirit world not to interfere with our memory photo. They gracefully stepped back, and we got our photograph of the physical people on the lawn.

Linda and I made many friends at the conference, and were invited to come back to Sweden. Over the next five years, the two of us travelled extensively throughout Europe. We had friends in each of the countries who arranged teaching seminars, healing workshops and private readings. We lectured, taught and did healing work, as well as many private readings.

Then in August of 1985, we traveled to Norway and stayed with a friend in Oslo. While there, we met a woman who was of Sami origin. The Sami people are indigenous to that part of the world. The Anglicized name they were given is the Laplanders, but they themselves don't use that term.

We met a Sami teacher and healer named Katya, who lived in the city and was more acculturated to European life than were her family members. When she heard that Linda's biological father was Lakota Sioux, and that we both had Native American guides, she wanted to meet us. She was interested in learning about cultural and spiritual similarities between the Sami people and the Lakota. She also sought an understanding of how Native people were regarded in the U.S., since the Sami were not well-respected in Norway.

Katya had a nephew, whom I'll call Tomah. Tomah was a shaman and walked with certain powers. Because many of the old ways had been lost, Tomah found himself living between worlds, serving as a kind of cultural interpreter.

One night, Linda and I were scheduled to do a mediumship demonstration at a local auditorium, and Tomah joined us. After the demonstration, Linda sang a Lakota song, as well as a couple of chants. Tomah agreed to do some Sami *yoik* singing. Like Lakota chants, yoiks are vocalizations from deep within the spirit of the singer that tell a story without the use of words.

When Tomah began his yoik, the sound pierced the air. The intonations were so tremendous they took my breath away. It was as though his voice shot an arrow of brilliant light directly into my third eye. That night, I could not get the light out of my head. I couldn't sleep. I was both hot and cold. I became quite ill for several days, lying on the heated tiles on the bathroom floor just to try and stay warm when the cold north wind passed through me.

Not only was my body in crisis, but also my spirit. It was as though gears that had been out of kilter were suddenly righted to the correct position, and clicked into place. Eventually, the light dimmed, or diffused, or else I incorporated it. All I know is that once the illness passed, I stood on new ground. To this day, when I close my eyes, I see that startling light.

I was subdued for the rest of the trip. I eventually regained my strength, but I knew I would never be the same. My understanding and acceptance of life had become more profound. I started to recognize that I was part of a greater plan that was developing.

In November, 1985, and again in 1986, Linda and I attended the Arthur Findlay College of Spiritualism and Psychic Sciences in Stansted, England. We participated in the college's Physical Phenomenon Week with Gordon Higginson, a world-renowned British Spiritualist medium and the principal of the Arthur Findlay College, as well as president of the Spiritualists' National Union of Great Britain. Gordon had trained as a young boy with his mother, the esteemed medium, Fanny Higginson, and then went on to train many of the most respected people in the field in England.

Gordon had sat daily with his mother learning how to attune to the spirit world. Fanny gave him everything he needed to live a life in service to the spirits. Apparently, it was foretold before his birth that this was his calling. So Fanny made sure that her son honed his gift as assuredly as a musician preparing to play on the world stage. Gordon aligned himself with his destiny to become one of the greatest mediums and teachers that the world has known. It was a great privilege to be in his presence and experience his connection to the spirit world.

On our first evening at Stansted Hall, Linda and I sat in the back of the packed library for a demonstration of mediumship. The energy in the chamber was alive, and the room fairly crackled with excitement and anticipation. People stirred in their seats, readjusting their positions, rubbing their legs, and shuffling their feet. It was difficult to settle down.

Gordon started giving evidential messages. At one point, he said that he had a spirit communicator who wished to speak with a Mrs. Jagodzinski. I stood up and said that Mrs. Jagodzinski was my mother.

"Please be sure to convey this message to her," he said. "Her dear friend Bob has just passed away from a heart condition. Bob wants your mother to know that he is doing well and did not die in vain. The valve they put in his heart did not save him, and neither did the other experimental procedures. But what the doctors learned is sure to help countless others. Tell your mother that he is thinking of her, and that as always, he sends his love."

My mother was deeply moved when I conveyed the message to her. Bob had transitioned to the spirit side of life the day before I received the message through Gordon. I was in transit to London at the time, and I didn't know that he had left his body. Mom did not work in any mediumistic capacity, but she had sat in séance circles with Linda and me and always appreciated the messages she received from loved ones. She never doubted the veracity of the spirit communications, or that life continued after death.

My mother and Bob had been close friends for a very long time. There were concerns about what the doctors did and whether they were using him simply for experimentation. The message that Bob was happy that the doctors learned something useful that could help others in the future helped my mother let go of any misgivings about his medical treatment and subsequent death.

During one afternoon session, Gordon asked the platform mediums to raise their hands. He pointed to me and asked me to come up with him.

My heart pounded as I stood side-by-side with Gordon Higginson.

"I'd like you to make a contact and give a message," he said.

But when I began to speak, he interrupted. "Your evidence doesn't include any names," he said. "I'd like you to try to deepen your attunement this time and reach for names."

I started again. This time, Gordon extended his auric field, the field of power in which he worked. Suddenly I found myself standing in that power with him.

I continued with the message, giving stunning evidence, including names. Not once did I stop or let my mind interfere. I kept going, immersed in the energetic field that vanquished all my fears and allowed me access to my clear, or clair, senses in a much more developed capacity. I stayed in the power with him and continued working until the power dwindled and he stopped me.

The grace and the beauty of being attuned so completely in that energetic field is a soul memory I could not forget even if I wanted to. By then I already knew that mediumship was my soul's path. Now I understood that my purpose here on the earth plane was to serve the spirits in whatever capacity they wanted. It was not up to me to decide. It was up to me to unfold in the spiritual power, and I would be guided every step of the way, without fail.

Another lecture was on apports, which I had never heard of, let alone seen. I'm sure my jaw dropped open as Gordon spoke about some of the objects that the spirits had materialized through various physical mediums, especially around Christmastime, at Stansted. Shells and other objects that the spirits had offered as materialized gifts were stored in jars at the hall. As improbable as it seemed, Gordon was quite certain that apports were real. So, he said, were asports, the dematerialization, or vanishing, of a material object.

Gordon explained that very few people are true physical mediums. It requires an individual who has the chemistry and the training to produce physical phenomenon. This type of medium may spend ten, or even twenty years, sitting consistently in a specialized development circle to produce objective results, that is, evidence that occurs outside the body or mind of the medium, and which all those present experience in the same way.

After dinner we gathered once again for the evening's demonstration. This involved Mr. Higginson's sitting in a cabinet and going into a trance-like state. A cabinet is used by physical mediums to condense or concentrate the energy. A great deal of concentrated energy is needed to produce certain phenomena. Sitting in a large, open room disperses the energy. A small, contained space condenses the energy, making it easier to use by the spirit world. It is a simple matter of physics.

Once Mr. Higginson was sufficiently entranced, his spirit controls could move his physical body. Depending on the work being done that evening, he might stay seated inside the cabinet with the curtain open, or he'd come out of the cabinet and walk around the stage. The room was dimly but sufficiently lit, and there was a red light to facilitate seeing what was happening. I should add that the curtain on the cabinet had been opened by a spirit helper, not a physical person.

Different guides began to speak through Gordon, especially Cuckoo and Paddy. Cuckoo was a young Black girl; her voice and personality were sunny and charming. Paddy, an older man who spoke with an Irish brogue, had a voice and personality all his own. Paddy acted in the role of master of ceremonies, but like Cuckoo, he spoke freely with those in attendance and gave spirit communication.

That evening, Paddy spoke to two roommates at the college. He recalled the exact conversation they had had an hour earlier about a search for needle and thread to repair the skirt that one of them was wearing. All they could find were a few safety pins to hold up the hem.

Then he said, "I believe this is what you were looking for. A mist of energy lingered in the air in front of the two women. Although the room was softly lit, we could all see a strand of at least a half dozen safety pins form in front of them.

"Put out your hand," he said to one of them. She did, and the collection of safety pins dropped out of thin air into her palm. "Now," he added playfully, "be careful what you speak about in your rooms!"

Everyone laughed, and the energy in the room became much lighter. The atmosphere of fear was gone. Now the spirits could get down to work. They had gained our trust.

Cuckoo and Paddy continued to speak throughout the evening, but Gordon's mouth never moved. It sounded as though the voices came from the side of his neck, or bounced around at a distance, independent of him.

The evening's events got even stranger, with a perfect white chrysanthemum forming and hovering in the air in front of a middle-aged woman who had lost her son when he was fourteen. Then it dropped into her lap. She was told to pick it up and hold it. Later, she explained that white chrysanthemums were the only flowers at her son's funeral. The casket was covered in them. The woman sobbed tears of joy. She now knew that her son lived beyond death, and that she would one day see him again.

From Gordon Higginson I learned that being a medium is not something we do, but rather who we are. Working with the spirits is a calling. It is a calling from deep within; it is a calling from our souls. Our souls call us to live a spiritual life whereby we can be of service to the spirits and to humanity. The spirits do not promise an easy life, but they do promise spiritual fulfillment. We are free to answer that calling or not. It is up to us how deep of a relationship we want to form with our guides and the spirit world.

Too soon, it was our last night at Stansted Hall. On both occasions that Linda and I were there, we stayed in the annex, a separate building down a footpath, away from the main hall. The last time we were there, there was an elderly gentleman named John in the room next to ours. John was very gracious, a gentleman in all regards. His wife of many years had crossed over to the spirit side of life, so he was at the college alone. He longed to hear from his wife, as she had been the love of his life.

Every night after dinner, we would return to the annex to change clothes before the evening demonstration. John would wait for us outside the building to escort us to the main building. By then it was getting dark, so he came prepared with a flashlight, not only for himself, but for us as well. Every evening he would guide us through the wooded path to the main Hall. Then again, at the end of the evening, he would wait for us and accompany us back to our room.

Once in the main building, we would go our separate ways, mingling with others who were there for the demonstration. John placed no demands on our time. He was simply there to make sure we made it safely back and forth between the buildings.

That night was different. The demonstration room in the main hall was pristine. It had been thoroughly cleaned and prepared. We were not let in until the appointed time, when we found seats near the front of the stage. Linda and I were in the second row, seated next to John. There was a definite air of expectancy.

Someone came out onto the stage and asked us to stay focused and to keep our thoughts directed toward the highest good. They reminded us not to make sudden moves or noises. This was years before people carried personal cell phones, but they were insistent that no one had a camera or recording device. The last thing they wanted was for a flash of light to go off from a camera.

We were also informed that Mr. Higginson had someone with him when he was getting dressed, who had conducted a thorough inspection. That person checked Gordon for pieces of muslin cloth, gauze or anything else that could be construed as excess material that could be used to defraud the audience. We were assured that what we were about to see would be the full workings of the spirit world, with no human intervention.

Mr. Higginson came on stage and entered the cabinet. Working as a medium in this capacity is a selfless and demanding task; it is not easy on the physical body. So the front row was filled with several well-known mediums whom Gordon sat with in his circle over the years. They were prepared to lend energy to the proceedings that night, to serve as spiritual batteries to help the medium. I understood that this night would be very different from the others.

Soon after Mr. Higginson went into trance, Cuckoo and Paddy spoke. Gordon remained in the cabinet, but Cuckoo was all over the place. First her voice came from one corner of the stage, and then the other. Finally, Paddy took over. He was a bit more solemn than usual. There was a lot going on both inside and outside the cabinet.

Because of my training and previous experience with trance mediumship, I knew that a lot of spirit people, guides, and spirit handlers in the room were preparing for what was to come. Although only one or two guides speak to the audience, there are many more working behind the scenes making numerous adjustments.

If you go to a concert, there is often a warm-up act. These are the actual people you see on stage, much like Paddy and Cuckoo. Behind the curtain is a host of sound, lighting and staging people, technicians moving knobs and handles on an enormous motherboard. Microphones are checked to ensure they are operating properly.

In a demonstration of physical mediumship, it is much the same. There are spirit technicians, who have worked with the medium for years, perhaps decades, getting to know them, understanding the faculty of their vocal cords, adjusting volume, syntax, and speech patterns. There is a long-standing relationship in which the medium and his, or her, spirit workers familiarize themselves with the other, learn what they can expect from the other, and what are their limits. This process of acclimatization is similar to making a friend. When you first meet someone, you may feel a certain chemistry, or shared interests. There is a learning curve in this budding friendship just as there is with our spirit colleagues.

The curtain to the cabinet was open. Gordon sat in there in full sight. A white, luminous substance, ectoplasm, started rolling out of him and onto the floor. It was like a waterfall of energy coming from his nose and mouth, and from his navel area. It billowed and collected much like soft serve ice cream.

The ectoplasm was fluid. It was pliable as it moved across the floor to the front of the stage. Invisible to the naked eye, spirit technicians gathered the ectoplasm together and molded it like elastic silly putty. They stretched it upward, pulling it like taffy. The slightly shimmering substance curled and rose until a form became clear.

The ectoplasm shaped itself into the form of a human being. I witnessed a full spirit materialization, not once, not twice, but several times that evening. Each time the spirit communicator gained a form, it began to speak to its loved one in attendance. Some of the spirit people were more fully formed and recognizable than others. Flesh tones and distinguishing features were apparent. People recognized those who came through. The atmosphere was one of hushed astonishment.

The last materialization was of John's wife. He held tightly onto my arm as his wife stood on stage and spoke with him. I think he held onto me out of sheer disbelief, coupled with utter amazement. In her delicate voice, his wife told him how deeply she loved him. She spoke a little about their life together. She did not want him to be so sad. She promised him that they would be together again.

With that, the energy dissipated. The form that was his wife became more amorphous. The energy that had built for the evening's demonstration waned. The row of powerhouse mediums, mostly women, in the front seats held their focus until the very end. With the demonstration coming to a close, they wanted to make sure that Gordon was well cared for.

The ectoplasm that exuded from Mr. Higginson's body, now had to be returned to him. This can be a risky business. If a stray pin, button, or staple was not cleaned up before the séance, and is on the ground as the ectoplasm rolls back to Gordon, it could go back into his physical body and endanger his health. It has happened with him, as well as with others.

The evening went well. Mr. Higginson was fine. He retired to his rooms. Amazed, we all went back to our quarters. John walked between us, holding on to each of our arms. He was so overcome with emotion that he could not speak. For the first time that week, it was we who made sure that *he* got safely back to his room.

There aren't adequate words to describe the impact of such an evening, such a week, or to convey the healing that took place. Hearts that suffered terrible losses were mended. Children, parents, friends, and lovers were reunited in a deeply personal and meaningful way. Souls that feared death were blessed with a glimpse of eternal life. They were restored not to faith, but the knowledge that life continues after the stage called death.

I consider myself blessed to have been in such close proximity to the spirit world. In the presence of Gordon Higginson, the veil between the worlds was lifted. Life and continued life joined hearts and minds to create tremendous healing for everyone involved. I never knew such things existed in the world. As I continued on my spiritual journey, one door led to another and yet another.

The privilege to be with and work with Gordon Higginson has been one of the greatest gifts and pleasures of my life. Being in Gordon's presence, and the presence of his guides, was destiny. He elevated my understanding of our relationship with the spirit world. He taught me about the delicate balance that exists between medium and spirit. Gordon brought respect, compassion, and unconditional love for the power of the spirit world. He fortified my commitment to my developing relationship with the spirits. He helped me to understand that together, medium and spirit co-create possibility and open the door to the blessings the spirit world confers on humanity.

Gordon Higginson transitioned to the spirit side of life in January of 1993. Since then, I have felt his presence and his help. As I write these words, I have the privilege of working with one of the well-known mediums Mr. Higginson hand-picked and worked with over the years, Colin Bates. It is Colin who suggested I write this story, and who has contributed the foreword for this book.

November, 1986, marked my last trip to the Arthur Findlay College. Far from leaving Spiritualism, however, I was broadening my understanding of the spirits and their world.

Figure 1.   Sitting astride Buttercup at Idle Hour Stables, Chicago, Illinois, in my first horse show, 1960.

Figure 2.   Riding Miss Confidence for a client at a show in Fond du Lac, Wisconsin, 1966.

Figure 3.   My grandmother and first mentor, Charlotte Jagodzinski, at Walt Disney World, Orlando, Florida, 1980.

Figure 4.   Deodi, left, and I at the Arthur Findlay College for the advancement of Spiritualism and Psychic Sciences, Stansted Mountfitchet, Essex, United Kingdom, 1986.

Figure 5. Deodi and I with transfiguration trance medium Queenie Nixon, at the Swampscott Church of Spiritualism, Swampscott, Massachusetts, early 1980s.

Figure 6. Lakota sweat lodge in Littleton, Massachusetts, mid-1980s.

Figure 7.   Grandpa Ellis Chipps, lineage holder for Woptura, in the shade of the ceremony house, Pine Ridge Reservation, South Dakota, 1989.

Figure 8.   Grandma Victoria Chipps, Pine Ridge Reservation, South Dakota, 1989.

Figure 9.   Deodi, Grandma Chipps and I at the Chipps camp, Pine Ridge Reservation, South Dakota, 1989.

Figure 10.   The Chipps camp, outside Wanblee, Jackson County, South Dakota, at the base of Eagle Nest Butte, mid-1980s.

Figure 11.   Students building a shade arbor, Pine Ridge Reservation, South Dakota, mid-1980s.

Figure 12.   Yuwipi man Godfrey Chipps and Lakota elder Wallace Black Elk, Pine Ridge Reservation, South Dakota, mid-1980s.

Figure 13.   Spiritual interpreter Godfrey Chipps with Bob "Ska" (Bob White), Godfrey's helper and fire tender, Pine Ridge Reservation, South Dakota, mid-1980s.

Figure 14.   Taking a breather during our auction of household goods, prior to moving from Kadoka, South Dakota, 1993. The Kadoka High School wrestling team moved everything onto the front lawn.

PART II

The Way of the Sacred Pipe

I remember what it was like to see the herds of buffalo crossing the plains, their hooves thundering, tearing up the grass as they went. This is what I saw when I was here on the earth plane. And now, this is how I see you, my dear children, as herds of beautiful buffalo crossing the plains. The buffalo were everything to us, they were our life. And you are everything to us. We love you as we loved them. We watch you grow. We watch you move through your lives. We watch you tear up the earth with your dreams and your desires. We cheer you on. We wish you the very best.

—My Lakota Spirit Guide

Chapter 7

First Nations

New vistas were opening, and the puzzle pieces of my life were like dominoes falling into place. My desire for spiritual growth was increasing. Fear of the unknown, fear of drinking and relapse, and fear of inadequacy were lessening their grip. I was able to breathe in more deeply, and in so doing my soul power was expanding.

My relationship with my guides, my spirit companions, was deepening. I was aware of them gently nudging me along. The spirits were always present, constantly reminding me of their great love. When I worked and opened the door to the spirit world, they were there. I committed to them, and they guided and taught me. We developed a working relationship, and I learned not to insist on having my way. This collaboration wasn't about the kind of work I wanted to do. It was what they wanted. They knew my temperament and abilities far more than I did. I trusted them to hold up their end of the bargain, and in turn, they trusted me.

In 1986, I attended my first Lakota sweat lodge. Then, Linda and I went to a gathering of elders on the East Coast, where we were introduced to Twylah Hurd Nitsch, a Seneca grandmother, elder of the Seneca nation, and head of the Seneca Wolf Clan Teaching Lodge. After we spent some time with her, Grandmother Twylah invited us to visit her on the Cattaraugus Reservation of the Seneca Nation of Indians, part of the Iroquois Confederacy in New York State.

Above all else, Twylah was a teacher. She was encouraging and loving to anyone who wanted to learn. The Wolf Clan taught the wisdom, the philosophy, and the prophecy of earth history. She believed that all creatures, as well as all of creation, are members of one family, that we share this earth with each other and all sentient life.

Twylah was a gracious and giving teacher. She invited Linda and me to stay with her in her house on the reservation. While there, we both fasted and did what the Seneca call a Clarity Vision. I felt honored to be on Seneca land and in the Wolf Clan ceremony house. Twylah spoke to us about her grandfather,

Moses Shongo, and his relationship to the wolves. She also spoke often about the Wolf Clan, and how the wolves are the teachers of the Earth.

"Wolves are both feared and respected," she said. "They represent the family. They are very nurturing and caring with their young. And it's not just the parents. The entire wolf pack raises and teaches the pups, and wolf fathers are as devoted to their young as the mothers. There is a hierarchy in the tribe with both a head male and head female. The other wolves respect their authority and wisdom, because everyone in a wolf pack knows their place and carries out their duties. So wolves are seen as teachers who show us how families can cooperate and work with each other as one."

We could only nod in half-understanding. What was there to say? This was as new a world as the world of Spiritualism had been to us just a few years before. All we could do at that point was to listen and learn.

Late one afternoon, I took a walk on the back part of Twylah's land. I was meandering through a muddy field when I felt as though a hand had reached up from the earth, grabbed my foot and ankle and yanked me to the ground.

There I was, sprawled out in the dirt half a mile from the house. At first, I was stunned, and then the pain exploded, shooting through my foot till the tears streamed. I wiped my face with a tissue from my pocket, took a few deep breaths and collected my thoughts. What was I going to do?

At last I found a sturdy stick and used it to hobble my way back to the house. When I told Twylah the story, she frowned.

"Can you tell me exactly where this happened?"

When I told her, she shook her head.

"I feel so bad about this," she said. "Where you fell down was where the natural gas line was cut off to the reservation." When she saw that I didn't understand, she continued, "Cattaraugus, the name of our reservation, translates to 'foul-smelling riverbank.' The source of that odor is the natural gas that oozes from the river mud and seeps up through cracks in the rocks. The gas company harnessed this natural gas, but they didn't extend it to us. My people have a lot of resentments about that, and those resentments are still festering under the land in that field. I'm really sorry."

That night, a friend of Twylah's happened to drop by. He told me that he was a bone doctor, a shaman, and he had come to treat me.

Seeing the look on my face, Grandmother Twylah said, "Don't worry. You're going to be fine. Albert is a medicine man, and his specialty is healing sprains, tears, and any problem that has to do with your bones. He'll fix you up."

I was receptive, but in truth, I didn't have much choice in the matter. My ankle by then was black, purple and swollen.

Albert gently took my foot into his hands. He neither pulled on it nor realigned it. Instead, he sang to it. With his eyes closed and the fragrant smoke rising from the herbs he used, Albert chanted vocables. Time disappeared as he sang, paused, rhythmically moved one hand over my foot, and continued chanting soothing sounds.

When he was done, I was extremely tired and went right to sleep. By morning, all the swelling and discoloration were gone. Whatever injury I'd incurred, it too had vanished. I was able to stand on my foot without any pain or assistance, so I put on my shoe and went downstairs for breakfast. In my work I'd heard about medicine people who carried different powers, but I'd never experienced them. I didn't understand completely, but I was extremely grateful for what Albert had done for me.

Grandmother Twylah was glad to see that I was no longer in pain.

"Now that that's over with," she said, "we have to do something about those trapped spirits and their resentment in the field back there."

"What do you mean?"

She smiled. "Soon, when the time is right, we will conduct healing ceremonies for the land, the people, the spirits, and all the resentments that still fester in that back field. It's time for a healing to take place for the land and the people of this reservation."

Now that I could walk again, it was time to undergo the clarity vision. This is different from a traditional vision quest in that the seeker doesn't need to do extensive preparations or undergo elaborate rituals. Rather than being about pursuing a vision as a spiritual life plan, its purpose is to find clarity around the seeker's life and path. That means that I wasn't meant to seek and implore the spirits, but instead go into the silence within and allow my innate wisdom to surface.

Grandmother Twylah's instructions were simple.

"The important thing is to keep your heart open and be sincere with your prayers," she said. "Pray and listen. Pray and listen. It's okay if you get tired and fall asleep. Don't worry about that. You could receive a special dream. Don't worry if you don't remember the dream. Someday, just when you need it, the dream will come to you."

Then Grandmother selected a fasting place for each of us. I entered into the teaching lodge with my pipe and water, but no food. For the next twenty-four hours, I stayed in that lodge considering my life up until that point, and asking for future guidance. It seemed that so far, I was on the right path.

On the last day of our visit, Twylah invited us to a ceremony in which we would become members of the Seneca Wolf Clan Teaching Lodge.

"Those who are a part of the clan have an obligation to teach others how to live in harmony with their own spirit and with each other," she said. "It will be your responsibility to share knowledge, but not only knowledge, to share wisdom. Above all else, you will be teachers, teachers of the sacred path.

Never forget that this is your purpose here on this earth walk, and beyond. All life is part of a sacred whole. You must cooperate with each other, and never forget that."

As part of the ceremony we received Wolf Clan teaching names. Twylah instructed us to use these names whenever we were in public, whenever we taught. If we used these names, we would remember that we are a part of the pack. We would always know our place in the pack. We would work in harmony to create one family, one world.

I was given the name Oshada, and Linda's new name was Deodi.

"Remember," Twylah told us. "Your names are a prayer. They will help you to remember who you are. They will help others to remember who they are. Both of your Wolf Clan names will bring nourishment to the people. The spirits will work through your names."

Within a month of leaving Twylah, we both stopped using our given names and became Oshada and Deodi. The names fit us as though they'd always been ours. It was as though Twylah had drawn out this hidden part of us. Now, Oshada is my name. It is my prayer. It is my path.

Around the same time, we met a man named Michael Harner, a respected shaman, anthropologist, and founder of the Foundation for Shamanic Studies. Michael taught classes in shamanism in Watertown, Massachusetts, and had devoted his life to studying shamanic cultures around the world. What he found was that many indigenous cultures had lost their traditional ceremonies. After years of dealing with missionaries, having their lands being misappropriated, and being forced to acculturate to varying degrees to the dominant culture, they had forgotten their sacred ways.

Although many shamanic cultures no longer had access to the healing ceremonies that once defined them, there were still threads that tied them to the old ways. The biggest challenge was that so many of their shamans and medicine people were no longer here on the earth plane to pass down the teachings that were so vital to their survival. In some cases, tribal members had no idea how to go directly to the power to gain the wisdom and medicine knowledge they needed.

Michael studied and lived with many of the still-active shamanic societies. He isolated common denominators in shamanic practices that ran across cultural and tribal lines. With this information, he created what he called Core shamanism. Core shamanism is a basic template for shamanic practices, which he developed from melding overlapping practices and ideologies from among the shamans with whom he lived and worked.

Michael's overriding goal was to bring these spiritual practices back to indigenous societies that had lost their shamanic practices. With this distilled version of shamanism, Native practitioners could journey to their ancestors, tribal elders and shamans in the spirit dimensions, in non-ordinary reality, to revive their own shamanic birthrights. As they were taught directly by their own medicine people from the other side, they could embellish Core shamanism with their own ceremonial traditions and rituals.

The Lakota have a word *wasichu*, which roughly translated means "he who takes the fat." Often, non-Native people come to indigenous people in need, or feigning friendship. Historically they have taken the fat, or the best, of the resources. In one Lakota story, the tribe prepared for the coming winter. The animals had agreed to give their lives so that the people could live through a severe winter, and their meat was prepared. While the meat was essential for the tribe to survive the winter, the fat was most highly prized, because it contained the essential nutrients for survival. One day, a half-starved Anglo man wandered into the encampment. Received with kindness, he was given a knife and told to cut off some of the meat. But he cut out only the fat and ate it. Because of this selfish man, the lives of the others were compromised.

Deodi and I could see from the beginning that Michael Harner was not a wasichu, and neither of us had any intention of being one, either. We began studying with Michael Harner. We wanted to expand our knowledge of the spirit world beyond the confines of Spiritualism. We wanted to integrate different cultural and spiritual practices into a unified whole. I had been an active medium, inspirational speaker and healer within the Spiritualist churches, traveling throughout Europe in this capacity. Eventually, I knew, I would come back to this path. But for now, I wanted to learn all I could about energy and the spirit world.

With Michael Harner, we learned about ordinary reality, OR, versus non-ordinary reality, or a shamanic state of consciousness, SSC. We came to understand that we lived in worlds within worlds within worlds. There were many levels through which we could perceive life.

"A shaman follows the rhythmic sound of the drum and journeys to the upper, middle, or lower world," he told us. "In so doing, we are in a shamanic state of consciousness. We always travel with the aid of our power animal, or animals, who not only escort us, but also work together with us.

If you are a native Chicagoan, say, and you have to go to a building at the corner of Randolph and State Street, you have a plan for how to get there. If you are familiar with the city, you know the route you will take. If you don't know the city that well, you get directions. Usually there will be two or three alternate routes for you to choose from. You decide which way to go based on the information you have been given.

"In the same way," he continued, "if you're a shaman and need to retrieve a lost soul part for your patient, based on your experience and the aid of your power animal, you know which world you have to enter. For example, you may know that you must journey to the fourth level of the lower world. If you're skilled, you already know the landscape in that world. You know what to expect. When you see certain creature beings or environmental markers, you are familiar with them. If you aren't, you rely on your power animal to lead you safely to where you are going."

There was a short pause. Then I said, "There's something I've been wondering, Michael. About voices. People often ask me what's the difference between when mediums hear voices and when people with mental illness do. And I know how to answer that. But what about shamans? Is it different?"

"Well, shamans see spirits and hear voices much like schizophrenics and other people who are mentally ill do," he said slowly. "The main difference is that shamans, unlike the mentally ill, can turn off their visions at will. Since their will, their training, and their specific work conditions open the door to the spirit world in the first place, they're also in charge of that door when they want the spirits to leave. And the spirits that work through them respect that relationship. But since the mentally ill don't control the door to the visions and voices, they can't close it at will, either. I certainly wouldn't recommend shamanic healing work to them."

I nodded. "Same with mediums, I guess."

"Absolutely. Mediums also need to have a solid grasp of this reality."

We studied with Michael and his associate Sandy Ingerman for three years, after which we were accepted into the advanced, three-year East Coast training program. On our first day of the program in October, 1989, Deodi and I walked into class and stopped dead in our tracks. There was Tomah, the Sami man who had sung his yoik and filled my head with such brilliant light, four years earlier.

"Tomah!" Deodi cried. "Remember us?"

"Of course!" he said, rushing up to greet us.

I could barely contain my excitement. Here was another sign that we were in the right place.

"So you're working with Michael Harner too, huh?" I asked.

He bowed his head and sighed. "I want to bring back the ancient shamanic practices to my people. Plus I want to make even close connections for myself with the spirit world."

The time we all spent together gave me a new world view. Working as a tight-knit group, we pushed limits in exploring other realities. I learned how to move in and out of different shamanic worlds and do healing work in an archetypal mode, where illness and obstructions could be seen in a representational way.

The group explored the terrain of the different worlds and mapped our personal landscape in the SSC worldview as it presented itself. We worked on each other doing retrievals and extractions, developing our craft. We became more familiar with charting the ins and outs of the upper, lower and middle worlds. We learned both trust and discernment, and that nothing is as it seems in OR.

An illness such as pneumonia might be viewed in non-ordinary reality as a large animal with a broken leg, unable to move, sitting on a person's chest. The task would then be to facilitate healing for the animal, so it could move of its own accord off of the patient. Within that vision, there could be layers of extraction and retrieval work necessary to facilitate that process.

Similarly, my twisted, swollen ankle on the Cattaraugus reservation might have been perceived as two snakes locked in combat, both tightening their grip on my ankle. Then there is the question as to why the snakes pulled me down to the ground and not someone else. In an SSC, I learned to work with power animals and allies to facilitate positive change in OR.

While taking our shamanic training to this new level, Deodi and I met a Lakota medicine family, the Chipps, who came to Massachusetts from Pine Ridge, South Dakota, to do sweat lodges and teaching. After two days of lodges and a healing ceremony, Grandma, the matriarch of the family, and her son Godfrey, who led the ceremonies, called us over for a talk. Godfrey explained that he had known of Deodi, who was adopted, and her biological father before he had ever met us, that the spirits told him about her and her father during a healing ceremony.

"That's why we came out East," he told us. "To find you and bring you back to the reservation."

Needless to say, we were stunned. Deodi knew that her father was Native American, and she had been pretty sure that he was Lakota. But she hadn't known much more than that.

For two years, we travelled back and forth to the Pine Ridge Reservation to learn from them. Then the family invited us to move to South Dakota. I was excited about going to Pine Ridge, but scared at the same time. All the shamanic training I had done up to that point was in a safe classroom, or contained, with Michael Harner right there in case any concerns came up. Now, Michael assured me that I could continue to count on him for help, but I knew it would be different.

We left the program with Michael's blessing and the gift of a buffalo robe.

"You're embarking on a rare opportunity," he told us. "This is a precious gift you've been offered. I really hope that you will stay there as long as you can. Stay unless your lives are in danger. Until then, learn whatever you can. Become the ceremonies. But remember, you have to know when to leave."

Michael continued to mentor me for several years. He told me I could be in touch with him any time. When I lived on the reservation, I wrote to him whenever difficulties came up, or if I had questions about how to handle specific situations. Each time he wrote back with suggestions and advice. Each time he would write, "Stay as long as you can. Stay unless your life is in danger." The advice seemed strange and a little frightening. But the longer I stayed on Pine Ridge, the more I understood exactly what he meant.

But at the time that he first said the words, I had to wonder. Until our lives are in danger? Know when to leave? What were we getting ourselves into? It was a long time before I fell asleep that night. I sat up in bed, holding tightly to the buffalo hide he had given us as a parting gift, and wondering if I was ready for the next step.

Chapter 8

South Dakota

When Deodi and I accepted the Chipps family's invitation to move to Pine Ridge, we had been working with a family that had a sick child. Because they weren't getting anywhere with Western medicine, they decided to join us on the trip to South Dakota. Maybe the Lakota ceremonies could help them.

The Chipps family lived in a reservation town on Pine Ridge called Wanblee. Most of the people who live there are members of the Oglala band of the Lakota Sioux Nation. In the Lakota language, *wanbli* is the word for eagle. Wanblee is located near the foot of Eagle's Nest Butte.

Ellis and Victoria (Grandpa and Grandma) and each of their sons who lived on the reservation—Charles, Phillip and Godfrey—had a government-issued home where wives, dozens of children and grandchildren lived. These homes, as well as the government-issued food served in them, were nothing you would want for yourself. Most reservation towns bear no resemblance to the outsiders' idealized version of Native life. Pine Ridge is one of the poorest reservations in the country. The extent of the blight was in plain view. Yet despite their marginalization, governmental abuses of power, broken treaties and enforced missionary work, the people have great heart.

It is said that the Black Hills, land that rightfully belongs to the Lakota Sioux Nation, is the heart of the nation, not just the Sioux Nation, but the entire United States. The great Midwest, where most of our food is grown, is commonly referred to as the heartland of America. If that is true, the Black Hills is where that heart beats. It is no great stretch to say that it is the beat of that heart, sounded by Lakota drummers, that keeps our nation spiritually alive.

When we arrived in Wanblee in 1987, life was thus a mixture of extreme poverty and great spiritual power. The Lakota have suffered for generations. Alcoholism, addiction, government housing, commodities, betrayal, violence, and babies having babies—these scourges existed side-by-side with a rich tradition of medicine men and powerful healing ceremonies. If you see the 1992 movie *Thunderheart* with Val Kilmer and Sam Shepard, you will see the town of Wanblee. The movie was partially filmed there. There is a heart-rending scene in which Kilmer and Shepard's characters drive through the town. As a matter of fact, they drive right past Godfrey Chipps' house. As they do so, Shepard says to Kilmer, "You've got the heart of the Third World right here in America."

For years, outsiders had come to the Lakota Sioux seeking answers. Some came to heal old wounds. Others were looking for cures for chronic diseases. Some came with sincerity in their hearts; others came as wasichus, to exploit the people and take what they could. There were even women who came looking to get pregnant by a medicine man, believing that this parentage would confer esteem and status on their lives.

Early on, we gained a deep respect for how the Lakota hold onto what still remains of their dignity and their land. There is power in the land, and there is power in the people. There is always a trade-off among the land, the ceremonies, and the people. Thus each person who comes to the reservation must learn the art of trading.

Deodi and I understood from the beginning that participating in tribal ceremonies inside an indigenous culture was significantly different from Core shamanism and Spiritualism. This was especially true of the medicine world of the Lakota. You do not enter into a situation like this and expect either the humans, or the spirits, to "play nice." There is a hierarchy of power combined with detailed ritual that must be honored. I knew that I was step-ping into a world that I had to respect from the outset, or there would be real-world consequences. It was not up to me to make suggestions, offer my opinion on how I thought ceremonies should be done, or take the initiative to do something better.

On our first trip to Wanblee, we rented a car in Denver and drove to South Dakota. I knew when we'd crossed onto reservation land, because I felt a shift in the energy throughout my entire being. It was as if we'd crossed an invisible spiritual boundary. Memories stirred inside me, and I could feel the change in topography in my bones and in my heart. I knew this land; this land, these people were already inside of me.

We came up and over one of the ridges by the buttes and took in the breath-taking, panoramic view of the prairie, with pronghorn antelope cavorting off in the distance. We pulled over onto a grassy knoll and stopped the car. I climbed out and stood spellbound, taking in the view. I breathed in deeply and filled my lungs with the scent of dust and fresh sage growing just a foot or two from my feet. I was stunned by the beauty as much as the familiarity, so moved that I got down on my hands and knees, touched my head to the ground, and kissed the earth. Tears of gratitude streamed down my face.

I have never before, or ever since, felt the urge to kiss the ground under-neath my feet. But that day, I knew beyond a doubt that somehow, I was home. I had found the one magical spot in all of creation that I felt inseparably connected to. My entire being resonated with this sacred ground. Although, in this lifetime, I had never been on Pine Ridge, I was as comforted standing there as I had once been in my grandmother's kitchen.

When I first met Grandpa Ellis Chipps, he was already moving away from this life and closer to the next. He and Grandma Victoria and their family lived in one of those government-issued houses. Made from inferior materials, they were also overcrowded. Walls were thin, plumbing quickly deteriorated with overuse, and there was no funding for maintenance or repairs. Basic hygiene was a struggle. In the same way, the government-issued food was overloaded with cheap carbohydrates, fat and salt.

Grandpa Ellis's grandfather was Woptura—Wope-too-kah—medicine man to Crazy Horse. Crazy Horse was a Lakota Warrior of the Oglala band, born in 1837. He had fought against the encroachment of white settlers on his Native lands in order to preserve his people's way of life. He was killed in custody at Fort Robinson, Nebraska, at the age of thirty-seven.

Woptura was born a *wicasa wakan*, a holy man, so recognized by his people. He walked with strong medicine. But the United States government suppressed the ancient ceremonies of the Lakota and forbade them to practice their healing rites. Crazy Horse, wearing medicine that Woptura made for him, fought tirelessly against the soldiers. Woptura's powers were irrefutable and his relationship with the spirits of the ceremonies unparalleled. It was through his vision that the ancient practice of the Yuwipi ceremony came back into being. This ceremony has defined the Lakota medicine man for generations.

The Chipps family name evolved over the generations. "Woptura" refers to crumbling chips of a buffalo horn, and of all things in life. The U.S. government did not know how to translate the name, so they assigned the family the name "Chips." Woptura had a son, Charles Horn Chips, who was a Yuwipi medicine man. Horn Chips' son, Ellis Chipps, was also a lineage medicine holder. (By now, the family had added a second "p" to the name.) Ellis's son, Benjamin Godfrey Chipps, known as Godfrey, or sometimes Ben, became the next lineage Yuwipi man. All these men walked with what are called "powers." The power they had was in their bloodline, and it was highly respected and sought after in curing ceremonies.

Outsiders lump medicine men into a single category, but there are hundreds of tribes across this nation and each has their own medicine men and women. Each tribe is distinct in their medicine ways and healing powers. The Lakota are known as being warriors and having strong, very strong medicine power. The Lakota have several different kinds of medicine men, and Godfrey

Chipps and his lineage are Yuwipi men. The Yuwipi ceremony deals with curing powers, a potent ceremonial healing ritual.

A Yuwipi man has a specific kind of healing power, and his connection to the spirits that work through him is strong, undeniable. The medicine man, his family, and the spirits all play their parts in the ceremony, with each knowing their exact role. A Yuwipi man does not work alone, his family is very much a part of the ceremonies.

During the Yuwipi ceremony, the medicine man is wrapped in a blanket, and is bound and tied using rawhide strips. He is laid, face down, on a bed of sage, barely able to breathe on his own. Once the ceremony begins and blackness envelops the room, the singing grows loud to welcome in the spirits who will do the healing. During the course of the ceremony, after the healing takes place, the spirits untie the medicine man, remove the blanket he is wrapped in, and throw it across the room to one of the participants in the ceremony as a healing blessing.

Early on, Grandma Chipps, as the matriarch of the family, told us what we were getting into.

"Among all the tribal nations," Grandma said, "we Lakota have always been known for our strong medicine. In our ceremonies, there is both a trade and cooperation with spirits. These spirits and powers work in an ancient relationship with the land and the medicine man. There is a balance that always needs to be maintained. Both sincerity and doing the ceremonies the exact way the spirits taught their human helpers to do them is very important. If things are done right, great healing takes place. But if mistakes are made, there is suffering."

Charles, Phillip, and Godfrey Chipps were all strong men in their thirties when I went to the reservation. I sat in Godfrey Chipps' ceremonies, also referred to as Yuwipi meetings, for many years. I witnessed the spirit power that worked through him. The spirits and the powers Godfrey walked with were not something ordinary men could handle. The relationship Godfrey and his ancestors had with the spirit world was something that needed to be nourished, through sacrifice, on a regular basis. Other medicine men, from different Native nations, came to the Chipps camp, asking the spirits to increase their powers, so that they, too, could have stronger healing medicine.

When other medicine men came, seeking stronger healing powers, sometimes the request was granted and sometimes it was not. Granting the request depended on what the spirits required of the person seeking powers. Some of the men who came walked away because what was being asked of them was not something they were willing to give in exchange for powers.

One such medicine man came to the Chipps camp with his entire family. When he requested stronger powers, he was told that he would have to do a fast on the hill. While he was fasting and praying, the spirits would look at him and his life. They would decide based on what they saw. They told him that if he had done more good in his life than harm, they would grant his request. However, if it was decided that he had done more harm than good, they, the spirits, would take his breath away. This medicine man decided that the risk was too great. He decided not to go to the hill and cry for powers.

Yuwipi men are instruments of the spirits. There is a different set of rules and expectations than with mediums, who serve as a channel for the spirits. Mediums focus their energies on the light, the great beneficence of the spirit world and their commitment to help humankind. The great ones work in collaboration with their spirit partners, who are constantly looking out for the well-being of their medium.

In contrast, Yuwipi men work to balance the light and dark forces to effect cures. A Yuwipi man trades with the spirit world: there is an exchange of energy, one thing for another. A Yuwipi man uses the raw power of nature and the universe, the type of power found in a bolt of lightning. In fact, he may actually hold a bolt of lightning in his hands, or at the very least be struck by one.

One day, Grandma and I were chopping vegetables when we got into a discussion of what it means to the Lakota to have powers.

"A Lakota medicine man is born with powers," she explained. "Being a Lakota Yuwipi man is a fact of nature, not simply a calling."

"Why did the power come to Godfrey?" Deodi asked. I hadn't noticed that she had been standing in the doorway to the kitchen; now she walked into the room and took a seat beside me. Like mine, her hair had grown longer since we'd been out west. Now it glistened in the harsh sunlight shining in from the window above her head.

Grandma handed her a knife and motioned to her to join us. "The power usually comes to rest with the eldest son, but it can be refused and passed down to another. That was the case with Godfrey."

"How did you know he had it?"

"As a young boy, Godfrey could disappear, or dematerialize. He came into his powers when he was about thirteen. He would walk through a wall and then materialize again on the other side."

Our eyes grew as big as hubcaps, and together we said, "Wow!"

But Grandma did not look pleased. "Of course I am very proud of my son, but I'm also worried about him. Because I know what is required of him. I know how disciplined he needs to be in order to harness and direct his powers. It hasn't been easy for him. It never is. But he's grown into his powers."

Feeling Grandma's concerns, I asked in all sincerity, "In what way has it been hard?"

"When a true medicine man is born to the Lakota," she said slowly, "the power is considered very carefully. It is not like winning some kind of prize.

Quite the opposite. It means a life of complete service. The child, once he is an adult, will have a meager life outside of the ceremonies. If the child and family agree to accept the power, the child belongs to the spirits. He will be raised within the family as normally as possible. We supported Godfrey, helping to nurture his powers as much as we could when he was young, but he already knew and understood things about us and about life that no one person should know at any age. For these men, the powers are a tremendous burden, not a cause for joy and celebration. Certainly nothing to brag about. Each ceremony takes a piece of his life. And we all pay a price."

Deodi lowered her eyes and shook her head. "It's popular these days for people to say that they or their child is a medicine man. I've seen it in both Natives and non-Natives, trying to make a buck, to gain a name for themselves. To gain a following. You know self-proclaimed medicine men tell women that they could be healed of any ailment just by having sex with them, right?"

Grandma sighed. "You can usually tell that kind of medicine men because they give themselves fancy names. But most Lakota names are about humility and service, not power. They are about helping the people and all of life."

"To the Lakota, power does not mean dominance. In fact, it means the opposite of dominance. A true medicine man is not boastful or grandiose. He shrugs his shoulders when attention comes to him. A true medicine man like Godfrey walks with tremendous humility. Animals and small children recognize this meekness and kindness at once."

"I've noticed that," I said. "The other day I saw a mare wander out of the field to follow Godfrey around like a puppy dog. All she wanted was to be near him!"

"Yes," Grandma said. I've seen that with hawks and eagles, too. And the children won't leave him alone."

Ceremony season began after the first thunders pass overhead in the spring and ended when the first snow flew, usually at the end of October. During this time, Grandma, Grandpa and the boys left Wanblee to live in a trailer on government-allotted land that had been in the family for generations, known as the Chipps camp. Half a dozen miles into the countryside, it was deep inside the reserve, cradled next to Eagle's Nest Butte, and it defined their homeland. Apart from the trailer there was the old ceremony house, a cook shack, a small bedroom, a single hand pump and a pair of outhouses.

I did not understand the dead seriousness of the ceremonies until sometime after that conversation, when I sat in my first ceremony with Godfrey. As usual, the family was in the ceremony room with him, to make sure everything was done correctly so that he would not be harmed. They held the power, sat with the pipe, sang the right songs, made sure the altar was set up correctly, the offerings were exact, the protocols were followed, the food was prepared properly, the right sage was gathered, and the purification had been carried out.

The altar was particularly important. The Yuwipi man's altar is the portal through which he leaves and then re-enters human consciousness and human space. Without his altar he would be lost in space, in a world where he could not live. The participants in the ceremony come as close to the edge of our world as our bodies and our psyches can tolerate. That's it, plain and simple. Except it's anything but plain and simple. It is an ancient process that few have the molecular structure for.

Not surprisingly, after each Yuwipi ceremony, Godfrey looked as though he had aged a dozen years.

The first time I sat in a Yuwipi ceremony in the hundred-year-old ceremony house on the Chipps land, I understood that the ancestors, the spirits of those who walked this road before, and the very land itself, rose up when summoned. This power was not a stream of white light and unconditional love. It was raw power that had to be harnessed. As impressive as Gordon Higginson's week of demonstrating physical phenomena was, this was different. What I was witnessing here was untamed power. Power that made no distinction between good and evil.

This was a shock to me. Again, I was as naïve as I was sincere. I believed that one had to be a good and honorable person, focused on spiritual evolution to work with the spirits. I had always associated truth, honor, and dignity with the privilege of being a medium. I saw myself as a channel for the light, and I believed that the channel was purified and made more holy as a result of the work. When I worked, my intent was always to raise my vibration to be in the company of spirit philosophers, guides, and healers. My intent was, and still is, to work from a place of love and compassion.

I knew that chemistry, and the proclivity to be a medium ran in my blood. I knew I inherited a gift, and I knew that gift was a part of my DNA. My innocence and inexperience led me to believe that because my gifts were enhanced by my dedication to truth and the highest good, the same was true of others.

Although I studied shamanism and became adept at it, shamanism was not, and is not, my first choice. In shamanism, the practitioner does battle with the forces of good and evil. I always wanted to work in the light. I associated my gifts with spirituality and God. Working as a medium has always been my first choice, my true love.

Gordon Higginson taught that a medium's first responsibility is to get close to God. The medium needs to unlock the Divine within themselves, and work in service for the greatest good in the universe. He believed that is the most important part of the training. He felt the specifics of training could come later, once that solid bond was cemented between medium and God.

I knew there were dark spirits. However, it never occurred to me that a person could have a dark heart and evil intentions and still have a relationship with the spirits. I mistakenly believed spiritual abilities were afforded by goodness of intention and heart. I did not understand raw power until I lived in a medicine camp. Power is power. It makes no distinction between good and bad.

Chapter 9

Ellie's Healing Ceremony

The healing ceremony for our young client Ellie was scheduled for the day after our arrival. Ellie had cognitive and language delays due to hearing difficulties, as well as constant ear infections that made her feverish and out of sorts. Because the ear infections suppressed her appetite, she was a fussy eater and had developed into a frail child. All of this made it difficult for her to relate to other children and have a semblance of a normal life. As a result, she was falling farther and farther behind in nearly every measure of physical and social growth.

Ellie's parents, Tom and Barbara, had taken her to a vast array of doctors, therapists and alternative practitioners, and each one had reached their own conclusions. By age five, she had endured more antibiotics and more scans than most adults a dozen times her age. We all hoped that Lakota medicine would be the cure that had eluded her.

It was no different for Tom and Barbara than for all the other families who put up ceremonies over the years. They were city people; their relationship with nature was limited to hiking in local parks or the occasional vacation in Vermont. They were not used to the manual labor required to set up a ceremony and were pushed to the breaking point more than once between struggling with outhouses and the extreme heat, cooking for two dozen people without running water, making prayer ties, and a thousand other chores—all while caring for three children.

The entire day was spent preparing for the evening ceremony. Phillip Chipps' medicine was his knowledge of the rituals and ceremonies. He knew exactly what prayers were needed, how many, in what order, what colors should be used, what altar, what directions, what songs, what and how many stones, what food, what tobacco, how many knots, what kind of knots, where they are placed, what kind of wood, which sage, which blankets, which, what, and how many of everything. If one element was wrong, not only wouldn't the ceremony work, but Godfrey could also be hurt.

The petitioners, that is, Ellie's family, had to engage in the preparations under Phillip's watchful eye. Others could volunteer, but the family could not ask for help. It was their ceremony, after all, and the spirits needed to know that they were sincere. Unaccustomed to the manual labor it took to set up a ceremony, Tom quickly succumbed to blisters and exhaustion.

As for Barbara, she had been raised in the city, as well. Cooking a feast for two dozen people without running water was no easy feat for her. Neither was struggling with outhouses, the extreme heat, and a crying child. Along with minding Ellie and her two other children, all this work pushed Barbara to the breaking point. Deodi and I volunteered to help her as much as we could, but physically we could only do so much. At the end of the day, we looked at each other with the same thought: We were just glad it wasn't our healing ceremony.

Little by little, we came to learn that the food used for the ceremonies— even the salt—could not be made with ingredients that were already being used for regular human consumption. Also, ceremony food could not be eaten ahead of time, or even tasted. If you so much as put your finger in your mouth after using it to wipe up a little splatter from the stew, you could not use that food for the ceremonies.

For the hundreds and hundreds of prayer ties required, Barbara had to choose fabric in the appropriate colors and cut it into little squares, which she then filled with a pinch of tobacco and strung together. Then, she rolled them together into large balls of prayer ties. There was an exact number of these prayer bundles for each color. When you were done, they had to be counted and re-counted many times because the number had to be exact—or else. And Heaven forbid if the cloth, the string, or the tobacco Barbara bought at the five-and-ten in Rapid City wasn't correctly steamed and purified—or even if the girl who cut and sold the cloth was on her moon time. In that case, the girl's menstruating energy would disrupt her intentions, and thus the material needed to be purified. Or maybe it couldn't be used at all.

Part of what made the experience so frustrating was that nothing was clearly spelled out. Tom and Barbara could ask for guidance on how to pre-pare properly, but then they had to offer something in exchange. Even then, questions were often left half-answered, and the rest was left for them to discover. I felt for them. This couple was at their wits' end.

When I asked Grandma what was the point of putting them through this, she told me to ask Phillip. He didn't hesitate for a moment.

"Why should we help them?" he asked. "They are already on our land, in our home, asking my brother to give up a part of his life by going to the spir-its, so that their daughter's life can be better. No one is under any obligation to teach or instruct them."

"But it's not like there's a guidebook," I said, as politely as I could. "How will they learn the rules?"

His response was brief. "They must humble themselves so that others will be moved to help them—not only us, but also the spirits. That is the Lakota way."

When he saw I was sincerely struggling to understood, he took pity on me.

"Look," he said, "we Lakota are poor, and in the outside world, we are powerless. When you outsiders coming here for a ceremony crying and frustrated, it doesn't come close to the pain we've suffered for generations. We want you to understand our ways, and that takes time."

"Outsiders think they know better. They think, how difficult can it be? If we break a rule, who will be the wiser? How can it hurt if we use the wrong salt shaker? But it does. It makes all the difference to them, and to us."

I saw his point, and I slowly began to take in the hundreds of details of Godfrey's ceremonies. The color for the west was black. The north was red, and east and south were yellow and white respectively. Each of these colors needed to be strung in sequence to create a large ball of prayer ties, four hundred-and-five prayer bundles for each ceremony. The number signifies the four hundred-and- five animal nations that according to Lakota tradition live on Great Turtle Island, in North America. Each animal, and each direction, needed to be honored. In so doing, the medicine man asked them to intercede with the spirits on the petitioners' behalf.

Despite Phillip's explanations, I continued to feel bad for Barbara. It could take a dozen ceremonies before your fingers acquired the body memory necessary to hold, fill, twist and tie the little pouches of tobacco. If no one volunteered to help, you would never get them done in time.

"I can't help it," Barbara would say when something went wrong. "I'm too tired to be angry, but I feel so alone here that I just want to leave and never come back. Yesterday I thought I was on top of things, you know? Then somebody came into the kitchen and helped himself to a bowl of the buffalo stew I've spent all day preparing. When I said something, he just said, 'Oh, I didn't know it was ceremony food.' So now I have to make another stew. I love my daughter, but really, what the hell am I even doing here? I could be home in an air-conditioned house with indoor plumbing and electricity. Instead I'm killing myself in this barren dust bowl."

What could I say? Ceremonial life is a calling that is not for everyone. Most people come with high hopes and end up leaving well before they'd planned to. Ceremonial life had not come easy to me, either. I learned, ceremony by ceremony, from both my mistakes and those of others. There were many times I too broke down in tears, or was so frustrated that I wanted to leave. Sometimes, I would just walk off muttering, "Are you kidding, what the hell am I even doing here?" Like Barbara, I could not believe that after all the hard work I had put in, my efforts were not good enough. I'd tell myself that I didn't belong in the middle of this bleak wilderness, and that I could be back home in an air-conditioned house with running water and electricity.

But each time I felt that the life was too difficult, I would put my personal feelings aside and take responsibility for my mistakes. And in that way I earned a new teaching and a deeper understanding of the ceremonies and the sacred pipe. I would always come around. I'd hear an eagle cry overhead, or see an antelope grazing in the distance. And a voice would rise from inside me, encouraging me to stay, telling me what a rare opportunity this was, and reminding me that if it was too difficult, I could leave tomorrow.

"Go outside for a few minutes," I told Barbara. "Listen for an eagle cry or watch an antelope graze. You'll remember why you came. And if it's too hard, you can always leave."

She wiped away a tear and gave me a thin smile. "But I won't."

Finally, all the preparations for Ellie's ceremony were complete. Someone in the camp took pity on Barbara, and told her to put a sign on the pot of stew that said, in big letters, CEREMONY FOOD. All the other food had been covered with large black plastic trash bags and labeled the same way. The prayer ties were made, the cloth for the flags was ready, the necessary offerings had been gathered, and sage had been picked. Now, it was time to purify in the sweat lodge.

It was dusk, and the fire had been going for hours. All the wood used to heat the stones for the sweat lodge had burned to ash. The stones smoldered under the hot ash. They were cherry red, almost luminous. The fire keeper placed a few more pieces of wood on top, but the flames had already done their job.

The men went into one lodge with Godfrey, and the women entered another lodge with Grandma.

"Men and women never sweat together," Grandma said firmly, looking me squarely in the eyes. "If someone tells you that is a thing of the past, don't believe them. That is the old way, and it is the right way. The men have their own struggles and vulnerabilities, and the women have theirs. Each needs their own lodge to share their hearts and purify in their own way."

Although most sweat lodges have an opening to the east gate that honors the sunrise and the morning star, the Chipps' lodge opened to the west gate. In fact, everything in their medicine began in the west. The west is where we go in the stillness of the night to look at ourselves. The west is the place of courage. It is where we discover who we are and why we are here. It is the direction that prepares us for the rest of our journey.

Sitting in that lodge on Chipps land, I was deeply moved. I knew that I was part of something much bigger than myself, that sitting with Godfrey and his family in ceremony meant that we sat with the medicine of their lineage. Woptura. Horn Chips. Ellis Chipps. Victoria Lodgeskin Chipps. There was an unmistakable power that entered into all the ceremonies. It was the power of the ancestors.

Along with the others, I sat on Mother Earth, on top of a ground cover of sage I had picked in the foothills earlier that afternoon. How sweet it smelled! I was grateful to the Sage Nation for giving us their children and grandchildren for us to sit on in the lodge. Feeling the coolness of the sweet herb beneath me, I gave silent thanks for the comfort it would give me once the ceremony began and the steam curled up around the willow frame of the lodge.

Then Grandma interrupted my reverie. "It's going to be a good one," she said, with obvious joy. I knew that meant the sweat lodge was going to be hot. "Are you ready?"

I nodded. No one else spoke. Our heads were bowed in prayer and anticipation. Grandma poked her head outside the lodge flap and called to the fire keeper. "We're ready! Bring 'em in!"

Without entering the lodge, the fire tender used a pitchfork to set the first, fiery red stone in the pit in the center of the lodge. The dark womb momentarily lit up with the glow. That stone and all the others to follow received a greeting and an offering. The first stone honored the west, and that was where it was set into the pit. The second honored the north. The third stone honored the east, and the fourth honored the south. The fifth stone, placed in the center of the pit, honored the marriage of the above and the below, Grandfather Sky and Mother Earth, and the other ten or so were added randomly. This was different than in other sweat lodge traditions I'd seen, but it somehow touched a place of deep remembering within me.

Occasionally, the fire tender missed, and the stone landed on the edge of the pit. Sometimes Grandma rolled it into place with the antlers. Sometimes she simply used her hands.

The first time that happened, my eyes grew wide. I could not imagine that her hands weren't seared, but she proceeded calmly, as though nothing out of the ordinary had happened. I had actually seen this once before, not exactly the same thing, but something similar. I was at a medicine woman's house one time when she was stoking the fire in her wood stove. The fire poker wasn't moving the wood into the position she wanted, so she reached into the stove, picked up the burning log and moved it.

Grandma saw me looking at her and gave a little laugh. If I could have seen her face, I know she would have been winking at me, as well. I wasn't supposed to see her move the stone with her bare hand. It was an automatic reflex on her part. She usually remembered to use the antlers, especially in front of outsiders, so as not to draw attention to her spiritual powers.

Later that evening, Grandma took me aside and said, "I don't want you girls making up stories about me. I've just lived here so long that the medicine from the land and the sky are a part of me. But I'm not a medicine woman." From the time I had already spent with Grandma, I knew that she was a remarkable woman who knew far more than she let on.

Meanwhile, those stones weren't just glowing. They were talking. They honestly looked alive. Staring into them, I saw faces and stories. I already knew they were waiting to tell me a story, but I had to earn the right to hear it. First, they had to bring me to my knees with my face buried in the sage. They had to make me beg for mercy. If I wanted to see and hear, I had to let go of my arrogance and be purified.

I knew what was coming next. All I could think about was how hot it would be when the first gourd full of cold water was poured on the rocks and they began to spit and steam. I reached back in order to finger the bottom of the tarps that covered the lodge, feeling for the slightest opening, that I could press my face up against when it got too hot to breathe. To my dismay, the lodge was securely fastened. Already the front of my legs and knees were turning red and felt burned. I had no idea how I would survive the heat.

Now, all of the stones that Grandma had called for were in the lodge. She told the fire tender to close the flap. He lowered the tarp and the blankets that sealed the door from the night air. Inside it was nearly pitch-black, with only the glowing stone pit in the very center of the lodge. The first dipper of cold water hit the stones, and the steam began to rise.

Prayers and song intermingled with the heat, but in my desperation, I could not sing, I could not find my breath. I wanted to throw up. I wanted to leave, but was tethered to my spot in the lodge. I sat directly across from the door, which is the hottest seat in the sweat lodge. When the air circulates, the heat of the lodge moves to the hot seat, or, as Grandma called it, the seat of honor.

From deep within the blistering heat and oppressive air, I heard Grandma's voice.

"Oshada," she called. "Oshada, put your head between your knees. Put your head between your knees. Ball up some sage and breathe through the sage. You're doing good. You'll be just fine."

How would I be okay if I couldn't breathe? And when I could, the air felt like it was burning my throat. But she was right, of course. Breathing through the sage did cool the air.

"I will be okay. I will be okay." I repeated the words to myself like a mantra. I knew that no one had ever died of asphyxiation in a lodge with Grandma. I hadn't heard of any reports of anyone melting to death or experiencing spontaneous combustion, either. I lowered my head to the ground to find some cooler air, but there didn't seem to be any.

Finally, I calmed down and simply prayed for strength to make it through the first round of the lodge. The penetrating heat brought up old psychological and spiritual pain. The physical pain I was experiencing mirrored the unresolved wounds I had been carrying around with me. My prayers quickly turned to tears that streamed down my cheeks. And the more I cried, the more I was able to tolerate the heat.

It felt like this first round lasted an eternity. But I had come to understand that what was being pulled out of me was all the grief and torment that I held onto since childhood. I began to wonder if it would ever end when, mercifully, there was a call to open the flap.

In seconds, the night air carried away the steam, and along with it the anguish I had released.

Grandma laughed. "That was a good one!" she said.

I took in as much cool air as my lungs could hold. Fortunately, my throat wasn't burned, and I could breathe easily. Grandma passed a gourd full of water to each of the women. Before drinking, everyone offered the water to Tunkasila, the grandfathers, and the above, in thanks for the gift of life. Then each woman touched the dipper to the ground, offering a little of the water to Unci, Grandmother Earth. Finally, after acknowledging the above and the below, she drank, and shared her water with the woman next to her.

Along with everything else, my relationship to water was being transformed in the lodge. Water plays a significant role in Lakota ceremonies, so participants, those who follow the sacred pipe, develop a deep understanding and reverence for it. When thirsty, people drink a glass of *mni* (mi nee). But in ceremony, Grandma said, water is called *mni wiconi* (wi sho ni), sacred living water. Wiconi is the water that sustains life.

The cherry red stones were now an ashen gray, and I was relieved. I told myself the second round wouldn't be as hot as the first. Then, just before closing the flap on the lodge, Grandma called to the fire tender and asked him to bring in six more stones. The bright red stones sat on top of the others, searing my knees once again.

The flap was closed again, and I made my prayers strong. I was determined to endure the heat, sitting up this time. I grabbed several stalks of sage, stripped the sage off the stalks, and rolled it into a ball in between my hands. I used the sage ball as a filter to breathe through. It helped to cool the steam. Once again, the steam rose, and it was my turn to pray out loud. I could not breathe through my nose, so I didn't know if I could speak and breathe at the same time.

In the darkness of the lodge, Grandma threw a dipper full of cold water at my face. Her aim was perfect, and I gasped in shock. Then I felt relief, laughed with delight, and began to pray aloud. I felt grateful to be in the lodge with Grandma. I knew that this was a blessing and that somehow, I had earned the right to be there. I wasn't about to squander this opportunity by whining or letting my fear takeover. The more courage I had to look at myself and face my resistance, the less difficult it became to tolerate the heat. I thought of the car crash, and the voice telling me to let go completely. I realized that I could let go in the lodge. I didn't have to stay attached to my suffering.

With a laugh of pure joy, I began to pray aloud. I was so grateful that I was able to empty my heart and give voice to all I was feeling. When I was done, others gave voice to their hearts. And like before, tears bathed my face.

After the last woman prayed, we all cried, "*Ho, Mitakuye Oyassin*," meaning we are all related," and the flap was opened. This time, I was smiling.

Grandma touched her hand to her heart. She said, "When you pray real hard from here, the spirits take care of you."

I understood what she meant. I knew how deeply and sincerely I had been able to pray on this second round. The heat and the steam brought the words right out of me. I let go of my attachment to my discomfort and became one with my prayers.

Soon, the flap closed for the third round. No new stones were brought in. In spite of my breakthrough in the previous round, I was relieved. Once again, I believed this next round wouldn't be as hot. But the water had barely touched the stones before the heat was unbearable.

"It's okay to lie down," Grandma said. "It's going to be a hot one." If I could have crawled out through the back of the lodge I would have, but my fingers never found an opening. I was miserable, and now my fingers were scraped raw with slivers of sage stalks jammed under my nails.

Since I couldn't leave physically, I left mentally. I thought about jumping into a cool, refreshing lake, or standing under a cold shower. Then I realized that I was drenched in sweat. I could not believe the sweet smell coming from my body. It was nothing like when I sweated from exertion. I was being bathed clean, perfectly clean, and sweet-smelling. Thoughts of escaping to a bracing dip in a lake evaporated. Once again, some defense was released, and I sat straight up. I was completely in the moment when all of a sudden, I became aware of a presence beside me.

Grandma was aware of it, too. She stopped the prayers and welcomed the presence. She spoke at length to it in Lakota, her words intermixed with guttural chants known as vocables. I sensed that she was deeply attentive to what was being said. I knew that none of us were thinking about the heat, or about how much time was passing. We no longer cared.

Then, I felt the woolly coat of a buffalo, its massive presence, and I felt its hot breath on my skin, different from the heat radiating from the stones. I smelled the scent of sweetgrass on the creature's hot breath as it grazed my cheek. I heard it snort right in my ear. But I had no fear. I knew the buffalo was a spirit, even though its presence seemed so solid. I even found myself wondering how a being so large could fit inside the sweat lodge.

Again, Grandma spoke in Lakota to the buffalo, thanking it. Then, it was gone. I sat bolt upright, not daring to move, even though the flap was now open and the water was being passed around. I wanted to remember what it felt like to have a buffalo standing that close to me, to recall every detail. I wanted to place the feeling and the memory in my heart, to hold onto to it and never let it go.

When Grandma asked the fire keeper if there were any more stones, I didn't wince. Trust had replaced my fear. The fire keeper told Grandma that he had saved two cherry reds just for her.

She winked and said, "I hope so. Bring 'em in."

He put the first stone on the fork deposited it in the pit. Then the fork deposited the second one on the rim, right in front of me.

Grandma said, "Just roll it into the pit."

In that moment, the fear returned and coursed through my entire being. Grandma wanted me to move the stone with my bare hand?

Then she laughed and said, "I'm sorry; I forget sometimes. It's okay." She passed the antler to the woman sitting next to me. She told her to use the antler to roll the last stone into the pit. Then she retrieved the antler and adjusted the last two stones.

Again the flap closed. Water kissed the stones, and they began to hiss and steam. Now, the passion had left the stones. They were still hot, too hot for me to touch, but I didn't feel the sting. The steam mingled with my sweat, and I could breathe without ducking down to the ground.

Grandma had managed to pull the last bit of fear out of me. She had brought it right to the surface and laughed with delight. With the fear gone, there was no separation between me and the lodge. I was not fighting it any longer. I had let go. I was inside the ceremony.

Next, Grandma reached for the bucket and poured the rest of the water on the stones.

She said, "This one is for Oshada," and laughed. This time, so did I. The thing was, I no longer needed cooling off.

At last, we all called for the flap to open one final time. One by one we crawled out of the lodge into the cool night air. I had never felt so clean in my entire life. My skin was soft, and I smelled like sweetgrass, like buffalo grass. Grandma looked me over from head to toe. Except she wasn't looking at me, exactly; she was looking around me.

Nodding her head in approval, she murmured, "*Lela washte.*" Very good.

Before we could proceed, there was one more thing to do. The fire keeper had saved two stones, which he placed in a metal bucket. One of the men carried the bucket into the ceremony house. Another followed right behind him with a bucket of water and a ladle. When he poured the water, those final two stones steamed everything in the ceremony house.

Purified by the sweat lodge, we made our way into the ceremony house. The food had already been brought in. Covered in tinfoil, it was lined up about two feet in front of where the women would sit. The altar was set, the prayer ties were placed, the bed of sage was laid, the flags were in the proper place, the rope was coiled and waiting, and the blanket was folded and ready.

Used by generations of Chipps medicine men, the ceremony house was a simple wood plank structure that looked, frankly, like a strong wind could blow it over with one gust. Yet that old wood didn't rot nor budge. It remained, ceremony after ceremony, storm after storm. There was no electricity, although sometimes an old electrical cord was run in with a lightbulb attached to it. In short, it was a bare, exposed and unabashed building. There was no place, no possibility, for theatrics or props. All the special effects would come from the spirits.

The men and women lined up on opposite sides, their backs pressed up against the walls. The women tucked in their legs, so as not to touch the line of covered pots, pans and dishes that sat before them. Charles and Phillip sat up front on the men's side, with Ellie's father Tom next to Phillip. Grandma sat up front with the women, Barbara and Ellie alongside her. The other Lakota sat closer to the front of the room with the rest of us, in random order. Occasionally, Grandma would call for a specific person to come and sit with her up front.

Deodi and I watched and waited. We had never been to a Yuwipi meeting, and we had no idea what the healing ceremony would be like. We were expecting physical phenomena, but other than that, we could not begin to imagine what would take place. All we knew was that once we began, the room would be black as midnight. How would we know what was happening? We had no idea, but we were thrilled to be there.

At last, Godfrey approached the bed of sage and put his hands behind his back. Phillip reached for a length of rawhide and tied Godfrey's fingers and hands behind his back. Then the Chipps brothers draped a handmade Lakota Star quilt over him. The quilt represents honor and generosity. It is handmade, with the sections joined together to create an eight-point star. The pattern is inspired by the Morning Star, which is the last visible star before dawn. It unifies the connection between the living and those who have already made their journey to the spirit side of life. It also represents the path of the spirits.

Charles and Phillip deftly bound the quilt around Godfrey with rope. With each turn and movement, they tied a knot, until Godfrey was wrapped from head to ankles, and his entire body was crisscrossed with dozens of tight knots. His brothers tilted him forward, then picked him up and laid him face down on the bed of sage. I could not imagine how he could breathe in that position. Without even looking at her, I knew Deodi was thinking the same thing I was. We were both completely enthralled. This was a far cry from the cabinet used by Spiritualist mediums like Gordon Higginson.

Then, the room was sealed tight. There were no windows, and now the single door was bolted. Someone snuffed out the candle, and the room was, as promised, pitch black. Next, the singing began, with Grandma's voice rising above the rest, piercing the veil between the worlds. Next came the men's voices. At first, I could identify the individual tones and singers, especially Phillip, but soon the voices merged into one sound.

At the same time, tiny blue lights began to twinkle in the darkness, darting around the room.

"Those are the spirits," Grandma said. "Welcome them."

One of the lights hovered in front of me, and suddenly, out of nowhere, I started to sing. With the light, that is, the spirit, in front of me, I knew the words to the songs. I sang full voice in Lakota. What did I know of Lakota? I was amazed that I knew the words, but I didn't question. I just kept singing. The light moved over to Deodi, and she started singing in Lakota as well. The power started to build as the singing got louder.

Thank goodness for my Spiritualist training! Without my experience in the séance room with the occurrence of physical phenomena, I don't know how I would have handled what came next.

Suddenly, the ceremony house started to vibrate like the spin cycle of a washing machine. Then there was a rumble. It sounded as if a gang of bikers were riding Harley Davidsons around the perimeter of the ceremony house. I could hear them circling and circling, faster and faster. As the noise moved around the house, it felt and sounded like heavy chains being banged against the building. The din was so loud that I sang louder to drown it out, but the louder I sang, the louder the thunder, the motorcycles got.

The sound escalated, the singing got louder, and, instinctively, I understood that I was supposed to keep on singing. No matter what happened, I was supposed to keep on singing as loudly as I could. It was important not to break the sound, because the songs were prayers. Deodi and I just kept singing, as though we had known the words and melodies all our lives.

My body relaxed into this strange world. I didn't need to think. I just needed to let the sound and words move through me. A sense of peace enveloped me. My heart and my voice merged, and I found my footing in the ceremony. I was one of the front row ladies, just like the women at Stansted Hall who sat in the front row, lending their energy while Gordon Higginson sat in a deep trance state. I'd been thrown into this new ceremonial world in the deep end, and had learned to swim, it seemed, in no time. I was more grateful than I could say.

Now the spirits began to dance on the food. I could see them, alighting on the tinfoil covering each dish. Each time they darted down, the tinfoil made a noise. At first, I could not believe what I was seeing or hearing. No one else was near the food, and yet the tinfoil kept crackling like it was being jabbed. Later on, when the candle was lit, I saw how the tinfoil was dented, like fingers had been poking at it.

Then, Grandma spoke to Barbara, who sat beside her with Ellie curled up on her mother's lap, sound asleep despite all the noise. Grandma told Barbara to say her prayers for healing. We continued to sing, while the mother begged the spirits to take pity on her child and help her. The singing got louder, because it was not ours to hear the mother's supplications.

All at once, Godfrey's rattles left their resting spot on the altar and flew through the air. They went over to Barbara and Ellie and moved all around them, touching them as they danced and spun. The singing and the prayers continued until the quilt, which had been meticulously tied around Godfrey with knot after knot, flew through the air and landed in the lap of the woman sitting next to me. It was done. The ceremony was done. The healing for the child took place, and, Grandma explained that the woman who had the blanket thrown at her also received a healing.

Then, as if on cue, the singing stopped. Grandma prayed some more in Lakota before lighting the candle. I could see Godfrey seated, cross-legged, in the middle of the sage bed. He had been released from the blanket and rope, and he looked exhausted. Grandma lit the pipe and offered the first prayer of thanksgiving before passing it around the room for us to do the same. *Wopila Tunkasila, Unci, wopila, wopila. . . .* Thank you, Grandfather, Grandmother, thank you, thank you. . . . The "Wopila" was said deliberately, from deep within the chest. When it came to the handful of Anglos, still stunned from what had happened, we mostly cried and prayed a simple, heartfelt thank you.

Once the pipe was smoked out and returned to the altar, and we all had a chance to express our deepest gratitude, the feast began. For the next hour, we sat around eating meat stew, a special bean salad made for Deodi and me, who were vegetarian, bread, chips, and a traditional berry dish called *wojapi*. It was three in the morning when we filed out of the ceremony house and returned to our tents to sleep.

Except I was too stunned to sleep. I kept playing over the events of the evening in my mind. When I tried to reconstruct the songs I'd sung, I could only remember a word here and there. The rest was a vague, half-formed memory. No matter what I did, I could not retrieve the songs, nor did I understand what had happened. I was amazed, enormously grateful, and, to put it mildly, overwhelmed.

I'd seen all kinds of things in the seance room, but nothing like this. The phenomenon was so visceral. It both filled me with awe and, to be honest, scared me. When the ceremony house started to vibrate, I had had no idea what was happening. This wasn't like sitting in a séance room watching ectoplasm exude from Gordon Higginson, with the polite Irishman Paddy explaining what was taking place. I had been a part of this. I had been in the middle of a profound experience that, to this day, echoes deep within my heart. I had interacted with the spirit phenomena, participating with every fiber of my being, without guide or explanations.

Again, I was grateful for my previous experiences, because without them, I doubt I would have grasped the magnitude of what had occurred. Still, I had so many questions. My mind jumped from one thing to another as I recollected the sounds from that night.

"What was the sound like motorcycles roaring?" I had whispered to Grandma on the way to my tent.

"It was the sound of Thunder Beings entering the ceremony."

I had never heard the thunder of raw power, and thinking back on it, I felt both elated and apprehensive. Spiritual experiences, I knew, often bring the feeling of ecstasy. After a demanding day of preparation, being pushed to my personal limits in the lodge, having faced and released deep-seated fears, I had been able to sit in the power that Godfrey, his family, and their spirits had created during the ceremony. It was like sitting in the eye of a thunderstorm as the power passes through you. It was a privilege. It was a gift.

In Lakota culture, gifts come with responsibility, and this was the source of my apprehension. I did not know what would be expected of me going forward. With a shudder, I thought of Michael Harner's advice to stay as long as we could, unless our lives were in danger.

I brushed off the warning as best I could and made a conscious effort to ground myself. I felt energetic roots grow out of the base of my spine, down through my legs and feet, and deep into Mother Earth, where I felt safe and protected. At the same time, I took a ball of sage, rubbed it in my hands, and inhaled its penetrating fragrance. The best I could do, with the sun preparing to make its appearance for another blistering day, was to try to get a little sleep.

The next day, little Ellie was more alert. She spoke to her brothers in short sentences and ran around the camp like a normal child her age. Her ear infection had cleared up, and best of all, she was hungry. Ellie's parents were instructed to bring her back in the spring for another ceremony as a follow-up, just as with a medical doctor. As it turned out, Ellie continued to thrive, and her developmental challenges eased. Her speech difficulties disappeared, and she spoke fluently. After the follow-up ceremony, she continued to thrive and was able to rejoin her class in school in the fall.

Since Ellie's healing ceremony, I have come to understand that it is possible to cure even cancer and AIDS with the ceremonies. I have borne witness to these cures. I do not suggest that if you have a serious diagnosis, you should ignore medical protocols and search for an aboriginal medicine cure. What I am saying is that sickness and physical constraints push us all to consider the value of our life and good health. Illness and the fear of death force us to look at our own mortality.

As we do so, we realize that we are impermanent creatures facing the meaning of our humankind. It is up to each of us to come to terms with how we will deal with, or deny, what is at hand. It is up to us to choose how we will live our days on this great and good Mother Earth. Ceremonial intervention is not how most of us will overcome the pain and suffering in our lives. However, we are all related through our common humanity, and we are all destined to walk on this earth together, at this exact moment in time. The choices we make about how to develop our spiritual understanding of life affects not only us, but every other sentient being.

As I attended more healing ceremonies, I gradually acclimated to the power surges and the phenomena. I learned to sit within the power and use the songs, that is, the prayers, to ground myself. I needed to stay present in order to lend my power to the ceremony, so the spirits could do their work through Godfrey and his altar.

Strangely, I could never remember the ceremony songs when I wasn't in the midst of one, but I could always sing them when the time came. My soul understood the songs, and I accepted the opening that allowed me to sing them. I realized that our singing raised the vibrations, or the frequency, of our surroundings, so that the spirits were able to ride our voices into the ceremony house. If they wanted to borrow my voice for healing, I was more than happy to cooperate.

Little by little I stopped trying to remember the words to the songs. I stopped trying to hold on, and simply accepted what was happening. When it was over, when the power left, I let go. After all, it wasn't my power to hold on to. I was there to contribute, to do my part, so the ceremonies could be effective, and Godfrey would be safe.

Over the years, Grandma took pains to teach me a few songs, even writing them phonetically. I spent literally days learning them, and there are some I still remember. The problem is, although I love to sing, I can't carry a tune. In groups, so as not to embarrass myself, I usually just mouth the words.

In Lakota, however, my voice and tone are crystal clear. When I sing in Lakota, you can hear a pin drop. It seems to be a gift the spirits gave me. I don't know how else to explain it. Many times, before certain ceremonies began, someone would call for me to sing the opening prayer. And without qualms, I obliged.

Eventually, I discovered that thanks to the spirits, there were certain English hymns I could sing, as well. My beloved Deodi was an excellent trance worker, and I looked out for her when she was in a deep trance state. When she or any deep trance medium returns to the physical plane, they require a smooth transition so as not to be rattled, or even injured. After learning from the spirits in South Dakota, whenever Deodi came back from a deep trance state, I sang a beautiful hymn for her to ride back on to this world. To this day, I feel blessed for this spirit gift.

This then was my introduction to the Chipps camp and the world of Lakota Yuwipi ceremonies. A few days after Ellie's ceremony, Deodi and I returned to Massachusetts. We immediately started to plan our next trip to the reservation.

Chapter 10

Preparing to Fast

Before leaving South Dakota, I made a commitment to fast the following summer. That is to say, I made a pledge to do what is commonly known as a vision quest, or *hanbleceya*, one of the seven sacred ceremonies of the pipe. The word translates to "crying for a vision." In the Lakota tradition, it takes a full year to prepare for a vision quest. It's known as a fast because the petitioner consumes no food or water for a given period of time, usually one-to-four days and nights while praying for a vision or guidance.

The person seeking to fast needs a sponsor to guide, instruct, and actually place the petitioner out on the hill, that is, the Sacred Mountain. Charles Chipps agreed to be my sponsor.

"As your sponsor," he explained to me, "I will be connected with you as you are crying for a vision. I will watch over you through the spirits. They will tell me what is happening with you, whether you are in danger, or have maybe fallen asleep. They will also let me know if you received the vision you sought, and when it's time to bring you down."

"Crying?" I was struck by the word.

He shrugged. "That's how we refer to prayer. We say that we are going to cry for a vision. When we say 'cry,' it shows how deep the prayers must be. It does not mean sadness and tears. It means being stripped of food and water and deprived of sleep. It means a great need to speak with the spirits directly, convincing them that you are sincere, and that your heart is kind and good. It also means a great need to speak to the *tunkasila*, the grandfathers, and Wakan Tanka, the Great Spirit. And to align yourself with the Creator's will for you. It means that you have come in humility and sincerity, asking the spirits and the Creator to take pity on you and help you."

I nodded. "Is it all right if I ask you some more questions?"

"Of course." He sat back in his chair, looking past my shoulder, toward the distant hills.

"What do you mean by 'pity'? What will the spirits pity me for?"

This time, Charles didn't answer at once. It was as if he wanted to be even more careful than usual about choosing his words. After a minute or so, I thought maybe he hadn't heard me. I was about to ask again when he leaned forward and looked me squarely in the eyes.

"*Pity* is an important word to the Lakota," he said at last. "When we pray, when we cry for a vision, we make ourselves pitiful. For us, being pitiful is deep humility. When we beg the grandfathers and the grandmothers of Creation, we remind them that we are worthy of their assistance. We say, 'Grandfather, Grandmother, I am only a human being. Please take pity on me; I do not know better. Forgive me, I am only a two-legged. I am only a man. I am only a woman. I need your help.'"

Like him, I sat with this knowledge for a while. Then I asked, "Why do you call it a fast? I've always heard the term 'vision quest.'

I saw the hint of a smile flash across his handsome features.

"We Lakota are deeply connected to Mother Earth," he said slowly. "We speak from the heart. Vision quest is a good term for the public. But fasting, this is as old as our people. The word is very straightforward. Fast. No food, no water."

"One more thing," I said. "Why do you say 'going to the hill' instead of 'going to the Sacred Mountain'?

"This one is easy. To us, all land, all mountains are sacred. It would be like referring to a girl as a female girl. People would look at you strangely and wonder why you are saying that. Anyway, our mountains are not so high as some. You call them 'buttes.'"

It was my turn to smile.

"I like that," I said. "Very low-key. There's less fanfare and ego involved when you say 'I'm going to the hill to fast and cry,' rather than 'I'm going to the Sacred Mountain for a vision quest.'"

"If you say you are going to the hill to cry for a vision to a Lakota," he replied, "they will drop their eyes to the ground and say, 'I'll pray for you, sister.'"

I appreciated the humble approach. Like other medicine families, the Chipps had had to package and commodify their ways in order to endure. And I was part of the growing American subculture that was searching for meaning that the dominant culture could no longer provide. In an important way, we needed each other.

When I first made my pledge to fast, I started out, like others, with a rather romanticized idea of what was to transpire. It didn't take long for reality to intrude on my expectations. There is a saying in recovery: "Expectations are preconceived resentments." And yes, looking back, I wound up with an awful lot of resentments on my way to the hill. As I grappled with each of them, though, I let go a little more, and then a little more. I came to understand that letting go was my medicine. It was my salvation.

In the fifty-two weeks of preparation for going to the hill, I had a regimen of spiritual practices to undergo. I did weekly fasting, prayer, and meditation. I have heard it said that prayer is when we talk to God, and meditation is when God talks to us. Thankfully, I was trained in prayer and meditation and was more than comfortable with those practices. I had no problem spending a full day talking and listening to God.

I could also manage a day without food, but not without water. Of course this was all taking place in the climate-controlled comfort of my home in Swampscott. I had running water, electricity at the flip of a switch, and a refrigerator full of food to look forward to. I knew that the conditions of my real fast would not be quite so supportive.

Charles had made it very clear to me that doing a fast wasn't just about the time on the hill, but rather the entire process. Going to the hill was the culmination of the story, not its beginning or even its middle. The preparation, just like for the other ceremonies, was integral to the outcome. Another way to look at it: I wasn't going to spend a few days on the hill to try to convince the spirits and the Creator that I was sincere and worthy of a vision. I was spending an entire year doing so.

I spent that year not only practicing Lakota values, but also making them my own. Prayer, respect, caring, compassion, honesty, generosity, humility and wisdom. Throughout that year, these concepts were foremost in my mind, and, more important still, in my actions.

Hardest of all for me was the swearing. I knew I had to stop, but it was a lot harder than I'd expected! I'd never thought that vulgarity was a significant part of my vocabulary, but sometimes, certain words say it all.

"Shit!" I said one afternoon.

"Hey!" Deodi called out from the other room. "You're not supposed to say that, are you?"

"Of course not. But I just said 'damn' by mistake, and I got so mad!"

We laughed about that a long time, but for what I was trying to do, it was no joke.

The night before we left for the Chipps camp in June of 1988, I couldn't sleep. At 1 a.m., I flipped on the television, and there was Rod Serling introducing an old episode of "The Twilight Zone." I hadn't seen that show since I was a child, when I watched it every Friday evening. Back then, I was equal parts fascinated and terrified by the show, with its creepy music and sound effects. But I never saw it again after a particularly disturbing episode, when I became so hysterical that my mother forbade me to turn it on anymore. My grandfather, who lived downstairs, actually had to come up and shake me to get me to stop screaming, and I was terrified for weeks afterward.

So here I was, watching "The Twilight Zone" the night before setting out for a life-changing event, and I realized they were showing the exact episode that had triggered my childhood meltdown. The timing was incredible. Here we hadn't even left yet for the reservation, and I was already being confronted with my deepest fears.

In this particular episode, a woman sat in a hospital bed, her face covered with bandages. She had gone in for plastic surgery, because her face had been terribly disfigured. She desperately hoped that the doctors and nurses could make her beautiful.

Her anxiety increased as the time approached when the bandages would be removed. Finally, the day came, and there she was, a classic beauty. But when she took the hand mirror a nurse offered her, she let out a wail. The surgery hadn't worked. But how was this possible, when she was so lovely? Then we see the faces of the doctors and nurses—all with distorted, pig-like faces.

I really don't think it was a coincidence that I watched the same episode that night, more than thirty years later. Of course, the experience had lost all its power to terrify the adult me. But one of the things that happens during preparation for a fast on the hill is that all our fears come to the surface for us to face, one by one. Before that night, I had considered this would happen in more of a symbolic, allegorical sense than in actuality. Not for the first or last time during the process, I found that I was wrong.

The next morning, we set out for South Dakota and Pine Ridge. That first night, we camped on the prairie with no running water and unrelenting heat, and two communal outhouses. It was a far cry from the comforts of home. After a few nights of having to pump and carry all our water, not to mention sleep with coyotes sniffing around the tent in the middle of the night, we had a good idea of what we were in for.

In fact, simply providing for our basic physical needs occupied much of each day. Putting up a tent in the interior of the reservation wasn't like camping at a state park, with shaded campsites and luxury facilities, such as bathrooms. The water situation in particular took its toll on me. Every necessity, whether brushing my teeth or preparing a meal, became an event that required meticulous planning. During the days in camp, there were always regular runs for food and gas. I usually volunteered for these missions, because it meant being able to wash up in a public bathroom at the market or gas station. I admit: I am a big fan of running water and toilets that flush.

Then there was the heat. The men in camp used trees to build shade arbors, simple two-sided structures with a crisscross of branches on top, so you could lay fresh pines across them. The shade arbors spared us from the direct sunlight and provided respite from the worst of the afternoon, when temperatures often exceeded a hundred degrees. At least there was no humidity, so even a little protection from the sun made it bearable. The only place we sweated was in the sweat lodge, because otherwise the extreme dry heat wicked away perspiration as soon as it appeared. Of course, we had to make sure that we drank enough water so as not to become dehydrated. So once again, we were back to the water. *Mni wiconi*. Water is life.

All of this was a shock to my system, both physically and emotionally. The divide between the spiritual richness and knowledge of the Chipps family and their physical impoverishment was painful to observe, much less experience. Yet for most, their hearts were so tied to the land that they couldn't bear to leave. Besides, if they did go to the city, how would they make a living? This meant that life was a delicate balance between survival and ceremony.

Through it all, I could never forget that I was there by my own volition and could leave at any time. When life became too grimy and oppressive, Deodi and I could go home to a different and privileged life. At the very least, we could go into Rapid City for a couple of nights, stay in an air-conditioned motel, watch TV while guzzling cold sodas, munching potato chips, and eat in restaurants. Our commitment was so strong that we never did, but still, we had choices. Our hosts did not.

Every day, an endless stream of people, both Native and non-Native, American and from abroad, arrived at the Chipps camp. Some would bring their entire families and settle for a few weeks, while others came alone or with a friend to stay just a couple of nights. They came for a variety of reasons that always involved one kind of ceremony or another. Some people wanted knowledge and guidance; others needed healing. Some were preparing to go to the hill; some came seeking an enhancement of their own healing powers.

Because ceremonies took place several nights a week, there were always preparations that needed to be made. Those of us in camp for the summer fell into a routine. We knew what would be needed and made sure there were plenty of stones for the sweat lodges, never-ending stacks of firewood for the lodge fire pit, and bundles of freshly picked sage. I quickly got into the rhythm of doing what was necessary. Now that I knew that those coming for the ceremonies could not ask for help, I offered it as often as I could.

I spent most afternoons making strands of prayer ties with Grandma. It was mostly the women who gathered to make the ties. We sat in the shade of the ceremony house with our cloth and scissors spread out on the ground. In the beginning, my fingers were clumsy and couldn't hold the cloth and tobacco while tying the string. But after a while, they grew quite nimble. I got used to the cadenced pattern of talking, praying, and tying the little colored bundles filled with a pinch of tobacco.

Grandma would talk and teach, and then there were long periods of silence when we would pray. One of the things she talked about was how spiritually and culturally important tobacco is to First Nation peoples. It is considered a sacred gift given by the Creator and has been used ceremonially for hundreds, if not thousands, of years. A petitioner always offers a medicine man a gift of tobacco as a sign of respect when making a request. This tobacco is then offered in ceremony to the spirits.

She explained about the significance of the tobacco itself, as well as the smoke from the sacred pipe. How they are a direct connection to the spirit world and a strong form of protection. The smoke carries our prayers to the Creator, the grandparents, the four winds, and the four directions. Tiny, tobacco-filled prayer bundles are also prepared for the spirits to take directly during the ceremonies.

This tobacco was a combination of red willow bark referred to as *cansasa*, along with other herbs, berries, or leaves. It is not inhaled, but rather offered to the spirit world. It's not the same as commercial tobacco, nor is there an addictive or mind-altering element to it. Commercial loose tobacco is okay to use, as well. And of course Grandma always had a private stash of her favorite brand, Bull Durham.

If I wanted to make Grandma smile, I would give her several sacks of Bull Durham. It's a loosely packed tobacco packaged in little cloth bags with a drawstring. She believed in the curative powers of the tobacco, and she was proven right over and over. Once, when I carelessly sliced my arm open, she packed the wound with tobacco, then wrapped and tied it with a cloth.

Afterwards she said, "Now don't touch it. Leave it alone. You'll be as good as new in a few days."

Next she swept her gaze over my entire body, lifted her hand to flick off invisible intrusions from the energy field around me. At last she gave me a final once-over.

"Good," she said. "Now go." Sure enough, after a few days the wound was healed and never even left a scar. I saw her do the same thing with burns.

Sometimes the grandchildren sat with us and made the ties, but eventually they would lose interest and run off to play. The other women came and went, and most of the men putting up ceremonies did not have agile fingers, which meant that more tobacco ended up on the ground than in the little prayer bundles. So the men would offer to do the more physical work. But Grandma and I would stay hour after hour, dedicated to our work. When it was just the two of us, she would often teach me sweat lodge or pipe songs. Because she knew that I grasped the importance of even the smallest detail, she trusted that I was counting and making the prayer ties correctly.

Grandma had a special pair of dressmaker's knife-edge scissors that she practically guarded with her life. You need to cut a lot of cloth into little squares when you make thousands of prayers ties a week, and cheap or dull scissors make the job frustrating and nearly impossible. If I borrowed those scissors, I immediately gave them back to her.

Grandma had a dry sense of humor, and she loved to tease. One day, she looked up from her work and asked, "Oshada, where are my scissors?"

I shot her a quick look. "Grandma, I put them down on the ground next to you."

"Well, they're not here. What did you do with them?"

"Grandma, check under the cloth."

"They're not here. They don't have legs. They didn't run away. You must have done something with them."

My heart sank, and I fought the urge to whine. "I gave them back to you. I put them right next to you."

"No, you didn't! I'm never letting you use my scissors again."

Eventually, Grandma found the scissors under the folds in her skirt.

"Oh, here they are," she said, closing the matter.

We both laughed with relief, but each time we re-enacted this little ritual— and we did it a fair amount—I could never quite be sure whether or not she was serious. What I will say is that a depth of compassion grew between us. I had the sense that the frantic search for the scissors reflected Grandma's pain. She felt the sorrow each one of her sons carried, and she felt the ache of everyone who came requesting a ceremony. The prayer ties we made reflected the acknowledgement of the hurt everyone was carrying. Our dance with the scissors served to refocus my attention on the importance of the prayers.

Back then, these special scissors cost twenty-five dollars. Thirty-five years later, I still have the pair I bought for myself in Rapid City. They sit in their form-fitted, felt-covered nest inside a tattered silver box. No matter how des-perate I get for a pair of sharp scissors around the house, I never use them in my daily life. They are my ceremony scissors, and more importantly, they are my connection to Grandma Chipps. How would I feel if I were to lose them? I couldn't imagine.

It was during these long afternoons that Grandma and I built an under-standing that ran deep underground, like a stream that silently wends its way through rock and dried earth. There was a knowing, a kind of kinship that connected us. Deodi and I were both embraced by the Chipps' family, but Grandma and I had a bond because of those prayer ties. She knew she could count on me to work quickly and keep up with her. A love grew between us because, I believe, of our shared understanding of their importance.

I honestly have no words with which to adequately describe the love between Grandma and me. Grandma saw my heart and my sincerity, and I saw hers. On a greater plane of existence, I believe, Grandma and I had lived many lives together. But more than that, we shared a consistent love of the sacred throughout time. When you make bundles of four hundred and five prayer ties, it's easy to lose count and make mistakes. Grandma knew that I counted and prepared each bundle with the same love of the ceremonies and concern for Godfrey that she did. This was our connection.

While we made prayer ties, others hauled water and cooked for the evening's ceremony. The ceremony food was almost always the same, a meat stew made Indian-style, which meant for every fifteen pounds of meat, you used a small bag of carrots and an onion. There was always a token salad or pasta mixed with a can of peas for Deodi and me, and sandwiches, sweet buns or sheet cakes, and *wojapi*, Indian pudding, sweetened with sugar. Lots of sugar. That made everyone happy.

As evening approached, quiet descended on the camp. Most people took a little rest, because we knew we would be up until at least two a.m., and sometimes till dawn, depending on how long the ceremony lasted.

One night, Deodi and I lay in our tent, chatting.

"It's amazing how far and wide the Lakota reach is," she said. "I met people today from Europe, Canada, and all across the U.S."

"And each came with a serious condition or concern," I replied. "It's too bad not all of them can be helped."

"Well, most of them can." She rolled over. "People just don't understand how hard it is here. So they leave. They don't get that there's no free lunch. They need to put in the time and the work."

"The ones who get it though, wow. The man cured of cancer? The tumor removed from that woman's neck? And Ellie?"

She shook her head in amazement. "Don't forget that kid's cleft palette that was repaired."

We were silent for several seconds. Then she said, "It's really something that they don't charge for their ceremonies. People come with so many expectations, but they don't always understand that there's no free lunch."

"It's so different than it was," I replied. "In the old days, the medicine man and his family held ceremonies for relatives and other Native people who understood that there was never a charge, but that the medicine man and his family needed to eat. They would arrive with horses and cows, and enough food to feed the entire camp. And they were prepared to do a wopila, an enormous giveaway after the ceremony in thanksgiving. There was a natural flow and trade of services and commodities.

"Sometimes someone will still bring a couple of bags of groceries and a carton of cigarettes," I continued. "But Grandma told us how much more important it is to give than to receive in traditional Lakota culture."

She sighed. "Yeah, we say that in the dominant culture too, but they really live by that code."

"Hey, you know what Grandma told me?" I sat up. "In the Lakota version of a beauty contest, such as queen of the pow wow, or spokesperson for the tribe, the woman is selected not by her looks, but by her degree of compassion, caring, and generosity. The Lakota don't value a woman, or a man, for that matter, who looks good, who's gotten accolades and public success, but who isn't kind."

Truth be told, we needn't have worried quite so much about the Chipps' non-existent fee structure. Godfrey never turned anyone away who came for a healing ceremony, no matter how ill-equipped or ungenerous they were. The universe and ancestral spirits had an ingenious way of handling the situation. While the people in question were in camp, the refrigerator would suddenly break, and a new one was needed. Or the meat locker was out of commission, and the family really needed its own freezer. Sometimes, it was the car that was running on bald tires that had to be replaced. Eventually, no matter how resistant the supplicants were at first, they came to understand that it was their job to buy the appliance or the new set of tires. Of course, it had to be their idea.

This wasn't because the family wanted compensation, however. Godfrey was willing to go to great lengths regardless of what was given. He was an intercessor between human pain and suffering on one hand and the benevolence and power of the spirit doctors who worked through him on the other. We witnessed firsthand how that took its toll as his health and vitality deteriorated over the summer. Each of the ceremonies took a piece of him as, quite literally, he gave up a part of his life so that others could live.

The real reason Godfrey helped people do a proper giveaway was that it was always up to the spirits as to who received an actual healing and who did not. They knew who was sincere. The spirits that work with the Woptura lineage of medicine can see into a person's heart. The spirits, the intercessor and his family, work hard in the ceremonies. The spirits demand respect, not only for the spirit world, but also for their physical counterpart, the Yuwipi man.

Godfrey was always willing, but those who came for help had to be willing to go to the same lengths that he was.

One night, I saw what happened when someone put up a ceremony without expressing proper gratitude. The actual healing went to someone else present in the ceremony house that night. The spirits decided to doctor one of the helpers who tended the fire. They didn't waste the preparations and the energy that had been built; they just rewarded it elsewhere.

Another time, someone came for help who had not properly prepared, and he was healed.

"I don't understand," I said to Grandma the next day. "We got to know that guy. He thought this was all a joke. Why didn't the spirits see that?"

She shook her head. "Don't worry. They did. They are hoping he will have a change of heart and show his thanks."

Sure enough, he did not. And by the time the man was ready to leave camp, he was already in pain again. I didn't talk to him, but I heard that he told people this was proof that the medicine doesn't work.

I relayed this to Grandma, and she nodded.

"The healing is not about the physical sickness," she explained. "This is just the symptom. All sickness is about the soul. Our medicine heals a person's spirit. Then the symptoms can disappear. But if someone can't be generous, they make a commitment to the sickness of their soul. So naturally, the symptoms will come back."

The Lakota are practical, down-to-earth people. True medicine men are not boastful or grandiose. They are very humble and shrug their shoulders when attention is drawn to them. There is an old TV commercial for a heavy-duty cleaning product called Janitor in A Drum. Godfrey used to refer to himself sometimes as "a janitor with a drum." This is an example of Lakota humor. We always got a good laugh out of that one, because it completely demystified the job and the title of medicine man.

Anyone who understands the life and obligation of a medicine man, a Yuwipi man, understands that he is in fact a janitor who cleans up other people's misfortunes and messes. There is nothing glorified, or power-filled, in the thought of a medicine man being a janitor, but that is exactly who and what they are. They are the clean-up crew for humanity, and they have a front- row seat in the arena of human suffering.

June turned into July, and life settled into a routine with the ceremonies. With another month before my fast on the hill, it was time to face another deep-seated fear. Several things were causing my sense of dread. For one thing, I was terrified of snakes, and somehow, everyone in camp seemed to know that.

I was on my way to the outhouse one morning when someone called out, "Careful of the rattlesnakes in there!" When I said thank you, she continued, "Sometimes they crawl overhead on the rafters, and they can drop down on you when you're doing what you came to do."

Her friend tittered. "Or they can come out of the hole while you're standing there."

I decided that everyone was teasing me and having a good laugh at my expense. I made up my mind that they were doing this to desensitize me, to help me to deal with my fear. Then one day, I heard Grandma complain to someone about a rattlesnake near the outhouse, and a couple of the men went down to remove it.

"Don't worry," she told me afterward. "It's gone. And there's usually only one."

It was clear to me that she found the rattlesnake more of an annoyance than a real threat. I wished I could be as cavalier. My fear nearly paralyzed me, and it got to the point that I was reluctant to use the outhouse. It's not as though I'd seen a single snake since arriving in camp. It was just that the thought of a snake dropping down on me while in the latrine was unbearable. And knowing that people were laughing at me didn't help. I spent a lot of time trying to decide which was worse: snakes coming at me from above or below. For years afterwards, I had anxiety about snakes hiding under toilet seats.

Anyway, a few days later, Godfrey was taking a walk when he came across a four-foot bull snake. To the uninitiated, bull snakes can easily be mistaken for rattlers, although they have no rattle and are perfectly harmless. In fact, it's good to have a couple under your porch, because they are known for eating mice. Personally, I'd rather have a couple of cats.

So Godfrey returned to camp with a large bull snake wrapped around his arm. As he approached, he called out, "Where's Oshada? Somebody go get Oshada!"

Now this may not seem like a good demonstration of his compassion, but in fact, Godfrey was a kind and thoughtful man. He knew I had to face this fear before I went to the hill, or I would have to deal with it up there, alone. I understood too. I can't say I answered his call eagerly, but I did go out to meet him.

The minute I saw him in front of the ceremony house with that snake, I turned to stone.

"Jean?" he called. "Will you come over here and take this for Oshada?"

Jean, who was not afraid of snakes, reached for it. After asking her to sit with me until I was comfortable holding it, Godfrey walked off. Then Jean sat on a bench near the ceremony house. It took a few minutes for her to coax me to follow, but when at last I did, she demonstrated how harmless the creature was. In theory, I agreed. But only in theory.

We sat together for about an hour, and Jean talked about snakes, and the good they do in the world, such as how they support the environment. I nodded in agreement while the anxiety in my chest screamed at me, "Run, get the hell out of here!" I had never been that close to a snake for an extended period of time.

Jean was incredibly patient. She played with the snake and showed me how harmless it was. She was in no hurry. After all, for her, playing with the snake was far preferable to preparing food in an overheated makeshift kitchen. Little by little, I got used to the snake's presence, the way it slithered back and around and through her hands. Eventually, I touched it. To my amazement, it was not slimy, like I had imagined. It was dry and felt like patent leather. Eventually, reluctantly, I was able to pick up the snake and hold it myself.

I could not believe I was holding this undulating creature without fainting. I wasn't exactly comfortable, but I did it. I held the snake and let it move back and forth between my hands. I wasn't so much proud of myself as grateful. I was grateful to make peace with the snake nations in a safe and controlled environment.

Once the lesson was over, we released the snake beneath the ceremony house. Ironically, except for that one cooperative snake, I never saw another one in all the years I lived on South Dakota reservations.

The very next week, Charles said, "Let's go for a walk." I knew enough not to ask where. I also knew when I fell into step with him that there would be a teaching involved in this walk.

The Chipps camp is at the foot of Eagle's Nest Butte, and we started walking toward the outcropping. It was a considerable hike to the base of the hill, and as we reached it, Charles said, "Let's walk up to the top. There's something up there I want to show you."

My other big fear was the fear of heights. I can't climb higher than the third step on a ladder without getting woozy and terrified. My entire equilibrium gets thrown off, and I freeze. I am fairly sure Charles knew that, but he just kept walking. Hesitantly, but willingly, I followed, calling upon whatever courage I could muster. I trusted that somehow, I would find the mettle to keep going.

As we approached the foothills I looked up, took in a gulp of air, and immediately had trouble breathing. It was just a butte; nonetheless, it was a few stories high. But I chose to trust Charles, so I started climbing right behind him. Somehow, I knew that he wouldn't let anything happen to me.

On the climb up, I didn't have much trouble, because I was able to lean into the solid rock. That made me feel safe. It was only when we got to the top, and I had to stand upright with only my feet on the ground and nothing but air and sky 360 degrees around me, that, sure enough, I froze.

Charles stopped, too. "Do you know why it's called Eagle's Nest Butte?" I shook my head and uttered a faint "No."

"Well, the eagles come up here with their prey. It's flat, like a table up here. They circle the butte and drop their prey on the flat table. Then, they come down and eat."

Being taken here is a gift, I told myself. *This is special.*

The problem was, as interesting and special as this excursion was, I wasn't sure I would make it back down. Then, Charles pointed out the remaining bones of the animals the eagles had dropped onto the top of the butte.

I appreciate this, I thought. *I really do. It would have made a great story, maybe around the campfire. But I didn't need to be here.*

I was so scared that I was actually beginning to rethink my desire to fast and cry for a vision. I'd been called to make a pledge to fast, but apparently I had not fully understood what I had committed to

Then Charles turned to me. With a reassuring glance, he said, "You know, what you are doing is a really sacred thing. You aren't just doing this for yourself. You are doing this for the people, and all your ancestors. Not just yours, but mine too. One day you'll see, you'll understand what I mean."

That was all I needed to hear. Those words struck a chord of hope and certainty deep within me. In that moment, I understood that I had answered an invitation, that this was a baptism into a new, and greater, life. I would never be the same once I fulfilled my pledge. The spirits were watching me with every fear I faced, and every step I took. The spirits believed in me, Charles believed in me, Deodi and the rest of the family believed in me. In that moment, I found the courage to believe in myself. I found the willingness to move forward.

He said, "I want you to walk the length of the butte with me."

The top of the bluff is quite narrow, with parts not much wider than the width of a man's shoe, or so it seemed to me. But when Charles reached behind and gave me his hand, I took it, and together we walked the slender span of the butte. I have no idea why I trusted him that day, except to say I was following my instincts. I did not hesitate. I guess I figured I would be putting my life into his hands when he left me up on the hill for my fast, so I needed to be able to trust him before I got up there.

When we got to the narrowest part, Charles said, "Don't look down. Just look at me. Put one foot in front of the other, and don't hesitate. Keep coming. You'll be just fine."

I did exactly as he said. I held onto his hand and stared at the back of his head. He kept turning around to look at me with those piercing eyes, not seeming to be the least bit concerned about where his next footstep would land. Charles was a large man, who did not look the type to be especially nimble. But he was. I had the impression that he could have done this walk blindfolded.

Step by step, I followed Charles, and before long we were on the wide plane of the plateau. It wasn't until that moment that I was fully able to appreciate the beauty from this vantage point. The sky was an indescribable blue, and I was not separate from it. I was in the sky world; I was a part of the sky. For a moment, I was able to let go of the fear and breathe in the intoxicating air that surrounded me.

And then, just as I was experiencing this incredible connection with the sky world, I heard the cry of two eagles overhead. They were circling directly above us, and Charles shouted to them, *"Hau, kola! Mitakuye Oyassin!* Hello, friend! We are brothers!"

In unison, they dipped their inside wings in acknowledgement. I felt honored and blessed to be there witnessing this lack of separation between earth and sky. I was in the eagles' world, and I felt enormously privileged.

After that breathtaking moment in the heavens, I had to go back across the treacherous strip of granite, but this time it wasn't a problem. Holding tightly onto Charles' hand, I walked across the narrow sliver of rock. Calm and reassurance replaced fear and anxiety. Before long, we started our descent from Eagle's Nest Butte, never speaking a single word.

Once we got to the base of the butte, Charles turned to me, flashing an ear-to-ear grin and said, "Not bad."

Relief and amazement washed over me. I said, "Not bad at all."

I gave Charles a nod of thanks, and he returned it. No words were necessary. It was silence that was called for. We respected the stillness that surrounded us on the walk back to camp. Off in the distance, I could still hear the eagles' cry.

My fast on the hill was two weeks away, and camp was full. Each day, more and more people came out to the Chipps' land for sweat lodges and ceremonies. In the midst of it all, Godfrey would sometimes take a few days off to rest and replenish his strength. Sometimes, he would go on a bender just to forget. I came to understand that an alcoholic stupor and the oblivion it brought could be preferable to the inside knowledge he had of the depth of human suffering. As I'd seen before, at the end of a Yuwipi ceremony, Godfrey resembled an old man riddled with pain. A few days later, he would show up again looking like the man in his thirties that he actually was.

But as the summer progressed, Godfrey wasn't always able to bounce back as quickly. Sometimes he wouldn't even show up for ceremony. We would do the sweats, all the preparations, but there wouldn't always be a Yuwipi that night.

Although Grandma had told me from the beginning, I hadn't realized till that summer how Godfrey carried the weight of his family, his medicine lineage, and his people on his shoulders. Although spiritual commitments like this are arranged long before a medicine man's birth, on a human level, Godfrey had not asked for this gift, nor the responsibilities attached to it.

When I mentioned this to Grandma one afternoon while making prayer ties with her and Deodi, her face clouded.

"Godfrey has struggled with his calling and his obligations to the spirit world most of his adult life," she said. "Sometimes, he makes choices that keep him from doing the ceremonies and give him a reason to live like an ordinary man. He suffers from his choices, but it's all a part of his path. He wants his own life, apart from the ceremonies, but with a job like his, he has no choice. The spiritual and the personal are one."

"And yet," Deodi said thoughtfully, "I can see how medicine men like Godfrey are like janitors."

I nodded. "With a front-row seat in the arena of human suffering."

We all grew silent. The thought of that much responsibility was awe-inspiring.

Then I said, "It seems like just when I think I know him, Godfrey does something unexpected. It's as though there's a tension inside of him that requires constant management, and he's not always able to manage it in a good way." As it turned out, not long after that conversation, he was charged with drunk and disorderly conduct. Deodi and I had to post bail in order for him to perform his ceremonies that night.

"I think that enigmatic quality is common to medicine men," Deodi said. We looked at Grandma, who nodded.

"There is always a small group of family and supporters who look out for him," she said. "They take his anger and his burn-out. And if a mistake happens during a ceremony, they share in the responsibility. But don't worry about Godfrey. As he ages, he will come to a place of peace with his calling. It's in his blood."

By mid-July, people were camping further and further away from the single water pump, which made it harder to haul water. I heard that we were expecting another medicine man and his family to come and set up their own camp. I didn't know the details, but excitement crackled in the air.

At the same time, the weather got really strange. One day we had a hailstorm. Hailstones the size of softballs ripped the tents and dented the hoods of several cars. After that, some people left camp. At least there wasn't rain. In the summer, there was so little moisture that the ground was parched and cracked, and flooding would have been disastrous.

Then, one day, the wind picked up at an alarming speed, and we all knew it was going to be a big storm. Of course none of us, except Godfrey, knew exactly how big. Early that afternoon, he came to our tent.

"I think we should move this next to the trailer house for safety," Godfrey said, looking at Deodi.

We knew what he meant. Deodi was on her moontime, so she was not allowed into the ceremony house. Unfortunately, the ceremony house was the building that offered the best protection. The ceremony house had stood for more than one hundred years, so it wasn't going anywhere, regardless of what happened.

The trailer house was extra-long, perched on cement blocks about three hundred meters from the ceremony house. It was more of a broken-down, rusted-out structure than an actual house. Truthfully, it was more like a ton of scrap metal, and there wasn't any plumbing. But it was roomy, an escape from the blistering sun, and had an assortment of chairs, couches, beds, and windows you could open.

We emptied the tent and carried it over to where he told us to put it. The ground was so dry and hard, it was like driving the tent stakes into concrete. I tried using my shoe, but at last I gave up and went looking for a hammer.

"It's okay," Godfrey said. "Don't bother." And then I watched as he took a few seconds to collect himself, and then used his bare thumbs to push each stake deep into the earth.

My eyes grew wide in disbelief, and my own thumbs ached in sympathy. I am not a weak woman, and I knew how hard that ground was. I had seen before how he and the other members of his family acted as though the extraordinary things they did were nothing special. I thought back to the time Grandma had moved one of the searing stones in the sweat lodge with her bare hand. When they saw you watching them, they brushed off what had just happened. By now, I was expected to take these occurrences in stride, so I said nothing. But I will never forget that sight.

Although Grandma and Grandpa had a house in the camp, it had just two small rooms and poor ventilation, so it got unbearably hot in the summer. Instead, they spent their days in the trailer house, which had cross circulation, as well as Grandma's sewing machine. Godfrey sometimes stayed there during the ceremony season.

People went in and out of the trailer house frequently. I went in mostly to talk with Grandma, or to see what she was up to with her sewing machine. Several of the grandchildren were always running around camp, and they, too, were often in and out of the trailer house. It was a good gathering place, where we shared a lot of laughter and stories. Plus, on the side that faced the road, the trailer threw generous shade, so we often sat out there to make prayer ties.

Now that a serious storm was coming in fast, the family and several others went to ride it out in the ceremony house. I knew they were offering a pipe to mitigate the effects of the storm.

And there was Grandma, at the door of the ceremony house, looking at me and shouting above the wind, "Are you coming? We don't have much time!"

I hesitated. I wasn't sure what to do. We were taught that a woman's monthly moon time interferes with the ceremonies. Deodi couldn't go in to the ceremony house, which is why Godfrey moved our tent for protection. A woman's menses not only interferes with the ceremonies, but compromises her as well. At that time of the month, a woman is considered to be in her power, and her energy affects the power of the medicine. For the most part, the ceremonies are about healing, which means that during the course of the ceremony, something toxic and no longer needed is removed from the supplicant. While on her moon, a woman is more open and receptive than usual; therefore, she can take on what is being discharged from the petitioner.

Traditionally, women at this time of the month stay together in menstruation huts at a distance from the ceremony house, separated from society. It was a time of quiet reflection: We spent our days talking and sharing stories, cooking good food, and enjoying the treat of having men deliver buckets of water. It helped to know that we were not being shunned. In the Lakota culture, a woman is honored, and a woman's time of the month, like her body, is considered sacred. Women are considered to be more highly evolved than men, and anything connected to a woman's body is considered sacred. Think about it: Men bleed and they die, whereas a woman can bleed every month and live. Traditionally women make the greatest sacrifice possible when they give birth. When they bleed monthly, this is a reminder of their power and their sacrifice.

So what was I to do about Deodi during the impending storm? I thought about what an energy healer might say. Probably something like: "Well, she should go to the ceremony house and simply protect herself. She could use a white light or close down her chakras, so nothing can affect her."

But the ceremonies here are not that simple. They are not a matter of energy healing. There are powerful forces in motion, and this is why a genuine medicine man ages and sacrifices a part of his life in the ceremonies. This is also why a woman on her moon must step away from the ceremonies—and the ceremony house—and protect herself, and the medicine.

I felt caught in the middle, between two sides, two cultures. Godfrey assured Deodi that she would be protected. Grandma wanted me to come to the ceremony house along with the rest of the family. But how could I leave her out there?

In the meantime, the winds were rising in velocity every few seconds.

"You know we'll be really close by," I said.

"I'll be fine!" she assured me. With a laugh she added, "And I bet I'll sleep better than you, without everybody around to keep me awake!"

I responded with a thin laugh. I was worried, but there was nothing more I could do. I left to join the others, but I still couldn't bear the thought of leaving her alone. So I kept running back and forth, back and forth between her tent and the ceremony house. Godfrey said she would be secure, but I was scared. Our tent was flimsy compared to the rolling thunder and squalls. Finally, the gusts got so strong that I had no choice. I needed to take cover and decided on a compromise. I went inside the trailer house alongside the tent.

There I was, in the midst of the squall, alone in two thousand pounds of welded and galvanized steel perched on cement blocks. It seemed to me that I'd be safe, although come to think of it, no one had suggested that Deodi stay there. By now, the gusts were too strong to run across the yard to the ceremony house even if I'd wanted to. The sky quickly turned black and menacing, and I was nearly paralyzed with fright. The wind against the trailer house felt like I was in the midst of a stampeding herd of buffalo, and it sounded like I was sitting inside an airplane engine. We were on the wide-open prairie with the butte on the far side of the camp, so there was nothing to interfere with, or slow down, what was to come.

As the gale swept through the Chipps camp, the motor home began to move on its blocks. I felt *tate*, the wind, toying with it, rocking it back and forth. Before I knew what was happening, the squall lifted the mobile home off its blocks and turned it on its side. As the trailer started to rise with the force of the wind, I jumped out the open door, which was already two feet from the ground, hoping to clear the path of destruction.

I hadn't thought it through. It was terror and gut instinct that caused me to jump out the door, after which I was immediately knocked to the ground and pinned under the trailer. I could feel the weight of the thing on top of my body, and although it was oppressive, somehow it was bearable. Something was preventing me from being completely crushed.

I realized then that two days earlier, Phillip Chipps had gotten his motorcycle out of hock from the pawn shop. He was thrilled to have his bike back, and I had been for a spin on it. It was sitting outside the door of the trailer house, off to one side. The force of the trailer house being picked up and flipped over knocked Phillip's bike on its side, in the perfect position to save my life.

The curve of my spine and my skull were safely ensconced inside the open space made by the handlebars of the motorcycle. As a matter of fact, it was the bike itself that created a wedge that kept this massive steel death chamber from crushing me completely.

I remember lying on the ground and not being able to move. My mind flatlined. I was in shock. My body completely relaxed as I was held captive under the trailer house. It took a few moments before I even had an emotional response. When I did, fear flooded through every part of me, yet, somehow, I was okay. I felt no pain, just panic.

Once the hurricane tore through camp, the rains came and there was a torrential downpour. The earth was so parched that none of the rainwater was absorbed. As I lay there, trapped and unable to move, I was afraid that I was going to drown. My head was on the ground, with the left side of my face laying in the muddy soil. The water was accumulating quickly, and it already covered part of my face. I panicked at the thought of not being able to breathe.

Then, as suddenly as the storm came, it passed. The rain completely stopped, and the earth started to absorb some of the water. I laid there, too numb to cry, breathless. It hurt to breathe with the weight of the trailer house pressing down on me. Everything started to shift when the ground began to soften from the rain. The little give in the terrain made a world of difference for me. I was fully conscious, but had no real concept of my predicament. I was simply grateful that the rain had stopped and I wasn't going to drown.

Up to that point I had faced my fears, one by one. First, came my childhood fear of the people with distorted faces, and the deep feeling of betrayal. Then, my fear of snakes, followed by my fear of heights.

My final and worst fear was that of being buried alive, and here I was, pinned under an enormous steel structure with my face in the mud, barely able to breathe. My worst nightmare was playing out in this bizarre set of circumstances. My perception of life and the world became very small, but I was alive. I was breathing. Nothing seemed to be broken.

People started coming out of the ceremony house to see what had happened. One of the cooks found me first. I remember him screaming, "There's someone trapped under the trailer house!"

Godfrey, Charles, Phillip and Grandma emerged from the ceremony house. Deodi climbed out of her tent. To my relief, she was completely safe, because the mobile home had toppled over in the other direction. Everybody was talking all at once.

The cook said, "I don't know who's under there. Does anyone know who it is?"

I couldn't say a word. But that morning I'd borrowed Deodi's watch, and my left arm was sticking out from under the rubble.

I heard Deodi cry, "Oh my God, it's Oshada! She's wearing my watch!"

With that, there was a momentary hush. In seconds, several of the men and Deodi positioned themselves along the length of the trailer house. Then Godfrey said, "On my count, okay, one, two, three," and with that they tried to lift the wreckage off of me.

But it didn't budge.

The five of them regrouped. Godfrey said a prayer invoking spiritual aid. After the pause, they tried again to lift the heavy frame. With the help of the spirits, the four men and one woman managed to lift over a ton of steel a few inches off the ground. Then Charles and Phillip reached under the wreckage, grabbed me under my armpits, and pulled me out from under the collapsed trailer.

Phillip insisted on pulling me upright and to my feet. A nurse in camp who had run to the scene objected strongly to that. In the midst of a huge commotion, someone shouted, "Don't touch her! She's probably broken! Don't move her!"

In response, Phillip—with whom up to then I'd had little communication—Phillip—who drank too much—Phillip—whom I was a little afraid
of—barked, "SHUT UP!"

After that, no one made a sound. Phillip assumed complete control of the
situation, taking charge of the spiritual power that was available. I'd never
known him to be so persuasive, or so sure of himself. That day, a force moved
through Phillip that was unlike anything I had ever experienced. It was as if
on that July afternoon, all the heavens were listening and decided to move
through Phillip. It was as though he knew that he had a very small window of
time in which to work, and he did not want to squander it.

Phillip and Charles pulled me to my feet and held me up. At first, I
couldn't feel my feet or legs, so they simply dragged me forward. With each
step, Phillip thundered, "WALK! WALK! SEND IT ALL DOWN TO THE
EARTH. LET IT ALL GO. WALK! WALK!"

Phillip kept impressing the same words, over and over, on a part of me that
surpassed my conscious mind. His commanding voice was greater than any
fear or resistance I had. He spoke directly to my soul.

"WALK! WALK!"

To this day, I can hear his words ringing in my ears. I followed Phillip's
voice and his authority without opposition. I knew, without question or
doubt, that I could walk. And, within a few meters, I started to move on my
own power.

At first, I walked tentatively, with two six-foot men hoisting me up, but
soon, I was able to walk just fine. My legs never buckled or faltered and
haven't since that day. I have never had a problem with the side of my body
that took the brunt of the weight from the trailer house. The only sign of
damage to my body was, and still is, a curved, inch-long scar under my right
elbow where I was cut by a piece of flying glass.

But there was more. When Deodi saw that I was saved, she raised her arms
to the heavens to thank the spirits for their help. With that gesture, and her
arms outstretched, the sky opened, and a bolt of lightning flashed. The lightning bolt pierced Deodi's hand, travelled up to her elbow, turned around and
came back out her hand.

Of course I knew none of this at the time. I am told that while Phillip was
busy demanding that I walk, everyone else was staring in utter amazement
at Deodi. No one could believe what had just happened, except Godfrey,
and, of course, Grandma. Deodi withstood the jolt of power and, amazingly,
appeared to be okay. It wasn't until days later that she suffered from heat-
stroke and had to be treated at the hospital.

I don't remember much else about that day except, later that night, Grandma
sponsored a healing ceremony for us. She wanted to ensure that Deodi and I
were going to be well. When I say Grandma sponsored the ceremony, what I

mean is that she organized everyone to do all the work: the cooking, cleaning, and preparation, so all I had to do was show up. Deodi, still on her moon time, had to be doctored at a distance.

Both Grandma and the spirits took pity on us. I should point out that Grandma sponsoring a ceremony for us was no small thing. We were family. At the time, I did not fully realize the bond of love among Grandma, Deodi and myself. As I look back, I see more clearly the destiny and the deep sense of shared purpose, we three had.

After the storm, most of the camp was out of commission. Apparently Grandma's sewing machine had flown across the yard. The kitchen was a mess, and most of the food was lost. So that evening, instead of buffalo stew and wojapi for the ceremony food, we had bologna sandwiches, potato chips, and sweet buns filled with jelly.

It made no difference. The spirits doctored me and told Godfrey that I was going to be fine, not only physically, but emotionally, as well. All the trauma and fear dissipated when Phillip commanded me to walk. Then, it was lifted by the spirits that doctored me. I have never had any bad dreams or other suffering since the healing ceremony Godfrey did that night.

The spirits spoke to Godfrey about Deodi, as well. They said that she would recover from the lightning strike, but there were other things the spirits told him that Godfrey never said to either of us. That is how it was with the ceremonies; not everything the spirits told Godfrey was to be revealed. If I had questions, I learned to glance over at Grandma. Inevitably, she would drop her eyes and shake her head back and forth to indicate *No. Let it go.* Sometimes, later on, Grandma or Phillip would approach me and share some tidbit of information, but it was usually just the advice to be patient. Godfrey knew a lot of things about many people, much of which was meant for his ears alone. He never interfered. He watched, waited, and made an occasional suggestion. It was up to us to pay attention to these subtle suggestions and take the action we needed to take.

After the hurricane, Deodi and I left camp for a few days and checked into a small motel on the edge of the reservation. I'm not going to say I didn't feel a bit guilty, because we were able to leave, and the Chipps were not. But I needed to sleep on a bed with a mattress, not on a half-inch foam pad under my sleeping bag. I needed a little comfort, air-conditioning, and respite from the unrelenting sun. As for Deodi, she needed to stay in a darkened, air-conditioned room. All I remember about those days was that we both slept. A lot. Clearly we needed it.

After a few nights in the motel, we returned to camp. By then, there had been a massive clean-up campaign, with everybody pitching in to help. A salvage company had towed the trailer house away, and Grandma's old sewing machine along with it. Eventually, the long trailer house was replaced with a small camping trailer.

The encampment was up and running in a few days, but several of the visitors left after their own tents and belongings were destroyed. For a change, the camp was blessedly quiet. Life slowly returned to normal, except for the loss of the comfort and convenience of the trailer house. The ceremony house, incidentally, hadn't lost a plank.

Living on reservation land is a simple matter of adapt or perish. The Chipps family was accustomed to loss and disruption to their way of life, but we were not. That kind of loss and trauma was not a part of our day-to-day experiences. So why did we stay? It simply never occurred to us to leave the reservation, although perhaps it should have.

I hadn't forgotten Michael Harner's admonition: "Stay as long as you can. Stay unless, stay until, your lives are in danger." What happened certainly would qualify as our lives being in danger. I could have been squashed, broken in half like a bug underfoot. Deodi could have died from shock. But those things didn't happen. We both picked ourselves back up and continued on. It's just what we did.

I'm not sure why we stayed. The best I can say is that there was a sense of destiny unfolding that we were both aware of. It never occurred to us that we were gambling with our lives. We were both determined to continue our relationship with the family, the ceremonies, and the sacred pipe. If our sincerity and commitment were being tested, we accepted what had been doled out and moved on.

The quiet did not last long. Life continued, and a new cast of characters found their way to the Chipps' land, seeking help for whatever ailed them. The sweat lodges and ceremonies continued with only minor delays. With each new family, there were lessons to be faced and obstacles to be overcome that were tailor-made for them.

Every time someone requested a ceremony, their dilemmas started to externalize, and their struggles moved out into the surrounding physical world as a mirror for them to see. Each time that happened, it reflected something valuable back to them about their maladies. This was always the first step in the healing that was to come.

I began to see how it was different for everyone, how each person who came had to overcome a unique set of circumstances and personalized fears that held them back. Everyone who came for healing was always brought to the edge of their world and all that they were hanging on to. That was certainly true for me, facing each of my fears in succession. Each person who came had their own path to humility, and to make themselves pitiful to the spirits that would doctor them through Godfrey.

I came to understand how preparing for a ceremony was always a vulnerable process. Every illness and set of circumstances we live with is ours for a reason. Life is a classroom with distinctive lessons that, on some level, our souls chose. This is not about blame, but rather, responsibility. Ultimately, we are responsible for everything that shows up in our lives. So, when we petition for a change, when we ask a medicine man to intercede on our behalf to the spirits, we need to look at how we got into our present position.

There were no simple answers on Pine Ridge. When I came to this Lakota reservation and sought the help of Godfrey Chipps, I too had to look at myself and my motives. The Chipps medicine started in the west. The door to their lodge faced the west gate. When we enter the ceremonies it is through the west gate, it means that we are prepared to look at ourselves, let go of illusions, and seek the truth.

Day after day, I watched people as they prepared for their ceremonies. My own journey stirred a well of compassion in me for our common humanity and suffering. I continued to do what I could to help others find their way through the preparations for their ceremonies. And the more I participated in the ceremonies, the more closely I watched Godfrey and his family work with each person, the more I understood the common thread that runs through all of life. We are all the same. No life escapes suffering and loss, and bearing witness to another's pain hones our souls. It has the power to make us more compassionate.

The Lakota punctuate greetings, departures, and many aspects of life, with, "*Ho Mitakuye Oyassin.*" *Mitakuye Oyassin* acknowledges that we are all related here on this earth walk. All two-leggeds, all four-leggeds, the winged, the creepy crawlies, the grasses, trees, stone people, and every aspect of life is interrelated. To see ourselves as individuals is an illusion.

The ceremonies took our attention from our personal troubles and gave us a difficult set of external lessons to learn. In the process, others took pity on us. Other people, sometimes strangers, reached out to help because they, too, knew what it meant to suffer.

Those who live life from their hearts know that we are all connected. In the ceremonies, we sacrifice for each other and pray for our common good. The preparations and the heat of the sweat lodge remove our arrogance and reduce us to our most common denominator, our humanity.

In the aftermath of the trailer house incident, I did a lot of self-reflection. I thought about the value of my life and the resilience I seemed to possess. Time after time, I had emerged unscathed from what could have been, should have been, disastrous circumstances. I never thought of myself as strong in body or spirit, but I realized that I was.

I also had an inexplicable relationship with the spirit world. Unseen forces had repeatedly come to my aid, for reasons I didn't understand. All I knew was that the spirit world watched over me like a mother who continually pulls her child back from the brink of catastrophe. To say I felt blessed hardly begins to cover the depth of my gratitude.

Chapter 11

The Hill

At last, the time had come for me to make my final preparations to go to the hill. Every afternoon, after all the chores and clean-up were done, I sat with Grandma making prayer ties and flags, but this time, they were for me. I also gathered all the other things I would need. Grandma sat with me in the shade of the ceremony house, telling stories of Horn Chips, her father-in-law. The stories always began with her husband, Ellis.

"Long before your time," she began, "Ellis was a powerful singer in the ceremonies. Now, you just see him parked in his folding chair in the shade, usually right around here, staring out at the land. He doesn't need much; his life is simple."

I knew what she meant. Occasionally, you could have a brief conversation with him, but, for the most part, it was Grandma who gave him direction and took cues regarding his needs. Ellis was mostly gone by the time I met him. He lived in a different world, remembering the past and watching the prairie grasses dance in the wind. He remembered the old ways, and his father's medicine, which was some of the strongest ever on Pine Ridge. Then, sometimes, he would look up and acknowledge a spirit that came to visit with him. A big grin would spread over his lean face, and you could hear him say, "Yup, yup," and nod in affirmation. Even though his mind was letting go, he was no fool. He knew exactly what was going on, and occasionally would speak up about some detail of the ceremonies. The spirits kept him abreast of things, despite his deteriorated condition.

"Ellis has a relationship with the sky world," she continued. "He can talk with the clouds, the wind, and those winged ones who lived in the heavens. He understands them and works with them. Everyone knows he draws his power from Father Sky, and the *wakinyan oyate*, the thunder beings.

"Did you know that he has saved the camp more than once by splitting the clouds?" I shook my head. I didn't know what that meant, but Grandma was happy to share how her husband had saved family members' lives, and the camp, more than once, from an approaching storm like the one we had just survived. Grandpa had prayed with his pipe, and the storm clouds split apart. The dark vapors divided as they passed over the Chipps' and their neighbors' land, leaving a calm swath of neutral air down the middle between them. Eventually the storm clouds reunited and continued on their path of devastation.

I had never heard anything like it.

"Yesterday I heard him laughing," I said. "He thrust his chin up to the sky like he was absorbed in another world." She nodded. She knew her husband well.

"Finally," I continued. "I asked him what he was doing."

Grandma looked up from her scissors. "And what did he say?"

"He said, 'Listening.' I said, 'Listening for what?'" She watched me with an amused expression on her worn face. "He pointed out into the distance, and he said, 'Wait. They're coming.'

"I looked up and saw these soft, fluffy cumulus clouds. I was looking for faces and shapes in them, thinking a spirit form would appear. That's what I thought he was trying to show me. But he shook his head—just like you're doing now, Grandma. He said, 'See, they're all lined up. They'll be here soon.'"

"He listens to the wind and the clouds," she said, as if it were the most natural thing in the world. Of course to her, I guess it was.

"That's it. He told me that I had to pay attention to the wind and the clouds, that they'll talk to me if I'd take the time to listen. And then he laughed."

Grandma smiled. "That makes him happy."

"Well, anyway, I focused and I waited, although I wasn't sure for what, exactly. It didn't really matter, though. I liked sitting with him in silence."

"You know you can't get Grandpa to say something he's not ready to say. He's not as sociable as I am. Anyway, it's not the Lakota way, to spell everything out for you."

"I'm learning," I said. "I stood still and quieted my mind. I tried to become one with the clouds, to hear the whispers in the wind."

"Did it work?" She was looking down at her quick-moving hands.

"Of course not. I'm too impatient."

Our laughter rang across the prairie.

It was no coincidence that we were discussing that lesson, of course. I needed to pay attention to it since I was going to the hill soon. In camp, all the lessons and teachings were magnified, and I needed to be more aware. Grandpa wanted me to understand something about the world above, and I knew I had to be patient. I resigned myself to sit quietly, not question him any further, and wait.

Be still and wait. It sounds like the easiest thing a person can possibly do, and yet I was not raised with that concept. In Grandpa's world, there was no need to rush anything. Now more than ever, his soul was not bound by time. When you live in a ceaseless present as the Lakota do, a perpetual "here now," your mind doesn't wander. There is no past or future, no regrets or catalog of upcoming activity; the present satisfies all longings. As Grandpa was slowly transitioning from this world to the next, he lived his life moving back and forth between the two. It mattered even less than before where he was or how long he had to wait. His soul was moving away from time into unending life.

That day, Grandpa kept on looking, so I kept looking, too. We waited in silence until two dark specks appeared high up in the heavens. Grandpa smiled and said a few words in Lakota that I didn't understand, followed by a prayer of thanks.

"*Lela washte, Wopila Tunkasila.*" It's good, very good. Thank you, Grandfather."

The specks drew closer and closer, and I finally realized that they were two spotted eagles coming toward the butte. Grandpa nodded his head and gave me one of his grins.

"*Hoka hey,*" he said. It's a good day to die. Then he shuffled away.

Grandpa knew the eagles were coming when he saw the cumulus clouds line up, and he wanted me to see them. He knew they were riding the thermals, and he could sense the excitement in the wind. Because he was in harmony with them, he felt the airlift of the eagles, their acrobatic maneuvers. They were, after all, his brothers. His people had lived and performed ceremonies at the foot of Eagle's Nest Butte for more than a century.

As I replayed the memory in my mind, I looked up to see Grandma watching me.

"What?"

"Grandpa was waiting for a sign," she said, "and it came. That was his blessing to fast on the land that generations of his family held sacred. You needed the family's approval, Woptura and Crazy Horse, the birds and the other creatures, everyone. This family is watching out for you, and Grandpa just wanted to be sure that everyone agreed."

"He said, 'A good day to die.'" I half-smiled, half-grimaced. "Hoka hey."

"It's true that 'hoka hey' is what the warriors said when they rode into battle," she said. "But by now you know it's also said before a spiritual challenge. All it means is that you should have the courage to shed the old self, like a snake, so you can be reborn."

I would need courage to go to the hill. Up there, I would have to agree to let go of parts of myself that no longer supported me before the spirits would consider giving me a vision. But that wasn't all of it. If I were fortunate enough to receive a vision, I would then need the courage to go ahead and live it.

Now, the sweats were becoming easier for me. I learned how to withstand the scorching heat and the intense spit and hiss of the glowing stones, how to breathe even when the air was on fire from the steam. I was even able to find great comfort in the experience. I could sit upright, no longer needing to bury my face in the cool dirt underneath the sage. Grandma no longer threw dippers full of cold water at me from across the lodge. I could let go much quicker and feel the healing, rather than focus on the pain of my resistance.

During those long hot afternoons, Grandma told me how she loved the sweat lodge, how it was in her blood. Her maiden tribal name was Lodgeskin, after the hides and skins that cover the saplings of the lodge to protect it and contain the energy inside.

"In the lodge," she told me, "the steam that purifies our hearts and bodies is sacred. It is the breath of the grandfathers and grandmothers, and it has the power to heal. Inside the sweat lodge is sacred space. It is where we go to humble ourselves and pray."

I noted that when my people pray, they dress in their Sunday best.

She flashed me a look. "Of course, that is not our way," she said. "We women cover ourselves only with a simple, cotton shift. Our status in the outside world does not matter to the spirits."

I knew to trust Grandma on this subject. She understood the pipe and the lodge better than anyone. She was the pipe holder for both her husband and her son, and before that, her father-in-law, Horn Chips. Sometimes I would ask her a question about it, and she would say, "Go ask Godfrey." But I could tell by the twinkle in her eye that she knew the answer.

Grandma taught me what to look for when selecting good sweat lodge stones. The rocks had to be smooth and of a certain size. You didn't want them to split apart when they were in the fire; they had to stay whole so they could tell their story.

Several times during that period, the stones glowed so hotly in the lodge that they became translucent. Fascinated, I watched them come alive.

One evening in the sweat lodge, we had thanked the stones one by one as the fire keeper placed them in the pit, acknowledging our personal connection to them as always. Grandma spoke to the stones with the same tone someone might use with a beloved pet. She noted how happy one or another of them was to be in the lodge with us. From time to time, she pointed out lines and markings within the stones and shared a story about them.

At a certain point, Grandma said, "Oshada, look at that stone sitting in the north. See how there's a dark shadow on one side?" I strained and squinted until at last I too noticed a heaviness in the stone. Even though it was bright red and translucent from the fire, I could see a cloud moving through it.

"Yes!" I blurted. "Yes, I see it."

"You know what that means?" I shook my head. "That means there's going to be an early winter this year. There will be a heavy snow before Phillip's birthday in November. I'll have to tell him." Her prophecy, I am pleased to say, came to pass.

One time some people unexpectedly arrived in camp, but Grandma was as prepared as though she'd gotten a telegram.

"How did you know?" I asked.

"The stones told me they would come. The stones tell me a lot of things. Just because I don't say anything doesn't mean I don't know." She gave me one of her penetrating stares. "You know I don't always want to know the things they tell me. Who to trust. Who to avoid. Why do you think I get chest pains? Sometimes it's too much for me."

I swallowed. "Did the stones tell you to trust Deodi and me?"

Her eyes twinkled. "If they hadn't, do you think you'd be here now?"

She had a point.

The next day, the two of us took a walk. We had been loping along in a comfortable silence for some time when I asked, "Could you tell me more about the stones?"

She thought for a moment. Then she said, "We Lakota know that there is no separation among life forms, and that none has more value than any other. The stone people were the first people. They are called *Inyan Oyate*. The stone people are to be respected and treated as valued brothers and sisters. When you honor them as relatives, the stone people will reveal their secrets to you.

"These stones look ordinary to you now, something you would see in a river bed, or crumbled from the butte. But they are our prophets and our protectors. We can see a world with the help of the stone people. We can also save a life."

She had been walking, as she often did, with her eyes on the ground. Suddenly, she stopped, bent over, and picked up a flat white stone. I couldn't tell why it was special, but she carefully dusted off the surface dirt and spoke to it.

"Oshada," she called, "Come over here." I was at her side in an instant.

"Stones," she said slowly, "are a part of the earth's history. They are not just the history of the here and now. They carry knowledge that has traveled through time. This has been going on for millions of years. When stones crumble, they become dust that is carried across states and even continents. Hundreds of years later, they become stones again.

"The Stone Nation has the power to teach us where we come from, and where we are going. They have endured creation and re-creation."

Then she took my hand and put the stone she had found into it.

"Now. Close your hand and your eyes, open your heart and your ears, and listen."

I did as I was told. I felt impressions flash across my mind and heard voices that I could not understand. I told Grandma what I felt and heard.

She grunted her approval. "One day you'll understand what they are saying to you."

I went to put the stone in my pocket, but she stopped my hand.

"Oshada," she said gently. "We are not miners. Put that stone back where I took it from and offer it some tobacco. Thank it for the teachings it shared with you."

I reddened, but she touched my arm. "We are obligated to uphold the balance of nature," she said kindly. "You saw that we did not come empty-handed, without a pinch of tobacco, or some coins or buttons.

I gently returned the stone to the earth.

After a while, we came upon a field and stopped before long, thick stalks of sage. They looked to be over four feet tall, and the field was several yards in diameter.

Pointing to what were surely the tallest, proudest stalks on the prairie, she said, "In the case of the sage, you ask the grandparents' permission to take some of their children. You never pick the strongest stalks. Those are the grandparents. You always leave them intact to look after their tribe."

I must have looked confused, because she continued, "Walk up to them and acknowledge that they are the grandparents of the Sage Nation. Make an offering to them, and tell them you are here to gather some of their children and grandchildren for the ceremony. Ask for their blessing to take what you need. And be sure to leave something behind in exchange for what we are about to harvest."

I did what I was told. Maybe in front of someone else I would have felt foolish, talking to these plants. But there with Grandma, it all felt perfectly natural.

Grandma took the time to teach me the sweat lodge songs, and sometimes she would ask me to sing them with her. That brought me tremendous joy. It felt to me as if we had sung these same songs together for an eternity. There was a remembering inside of me that made me feel whole. If I could, I would have crawled inside the songs and stayed there forever, inside the vibration we were creating with our voices.

The Lakota sing their prayers. There is, of course, secular singing, like at the pow wows, but the ceremony songs are prayers. My favorite prayer is a song about remembering to pray. It's a purification song that honors the grandparents, and each of the directions, called *Cekiya Yo*.

> Look toward the West
> Your grandfather
> Is sitting there looking this way.

> Pray to Him! Pray to Him!

The song repeats the same words with each direction, and then ends:

> Look up above,
> The Great Spirit,
> He is sitting above us.
> Pray to Him! Pray to Him!
> He is sitting there looking this way
> Look down at the Earth,
> Your Grandmother
> Is lying beneath you.
> Pray to Her! Pray to Her!
> She is listening to your prayers.

I loved how the song demonstrates how the Lakota see all of life, including the directions, the standing nations—which is what they call trees—the sage and grass people, the hundreds of animal nations, the buttes, the vegetables in the garden, all of life as having grandparents that protect and care for them, like we do. The grandparents hold space for their children and grandchildren to flourish and must be acknowledged.

Here, with the Lakota, I could see so clearly how everything hinges on accepting our roles in the interconnectedness of life. How our prayers recognize and remind us that we are all connected. I understood intuitively that like the Lakota, my nation too stands stronger when it remembers these connections. In fact, all Grandma's teachings made sense to me on an instinctive level. I was a thirsty sponge, absorbing all the knowledge and customs like so much water.

I had come to the Chipps with an understanding that life was eternal, and that we lived on a continuum of experience as we passed from life through death though life through death though life. Now, I could see that there was something about these teachings that was already there, deep in my bones. Not for the first time, I felt I was home.

During those final two weeks, Grandma and I found ourselves sitting alone in the shade of the ceremony house more often than ever, our dancing fingers holding, pinching, folding, and tying the little bundles. Deodi was busy helping others to prepare for their ceremonies. The younger children no longer had any patience for it, while many of those who had come to request healing ceremonies didn't have the dexterity. But Grandma, and soon I, were so adapted to the routine, that we were quicker than anyone else. It got to the point that others would barter chores with me in exchange for those colored bundles.

One of the last days before my fast, Grandma fixed that all-seeing gaze on me, the one she used when she was being extra-serious.

"A few more things," she said. "You know you have to make all the ties and flags yourself. I want to make sure you have plenty of time to do that." I nodded. "And don't worry about the eagle feather." She leaned closer and grinned. "I have a special one set aside just for you. But don't tell anybody."

Sometimes, Phillip would come by and say a few words while we worked. He wasn't an easy man to know, but sometimes it was possible to bridge the gap between his porcupine exterior and his heart. I would forever be grateful for him for restoring the use of my legs.

After he sauntered off, Grandma clicked her tongue.

"That boy," she said, shaking her head. "He knows what is involved in the ceremonies better than anyone. We all rely on him, but Godfrey most of all."

"I was so surprised that he took an interest in me that day with the trailer," I said. "He would be the last person I would have thought to save me."

"It shows how much a part of this family you are. Apart from the ceremonies, he takes little interest in any of the people who come here. As you know, many who come do not make an effort to understand the seriousness of what they are asking. Phillip can sniff out these people quicker than anybody, and he will not give them a moment more of his time than he has to do. I think that more than his brothers, he is pained by being caught between reservation life and the rest of the world."

"It makes sense," I said. "He doesn't have power in the outside world, and in this world, as much as he defends the sacred rituals, he isn't a medicine man. No wonder he keeps to himself."

"He has a wild streak, that one," she said, brushing away a tear. "Life is hard, but he doesn't make it any easier on himself. None of them do."

I sighed. I knew she was talking about his substance abuse problem. Her voice held so much sorrow that I stopped my work for a moment to look more closely at her. Given my history, I wished with all my being that I could share my recovery with Phillip. But he needed an insider, a role model who understood his life and the problems that came with it.

As usual, I didn't need to say what I was thinking with Grandma.

"Yes, he has a problem with alcohol and drugs, and it makes him mean-spirited sometimes. But there's a kindness underneath."

"Oh yes," I said. "You can see it in his eyes."

"I often think that if Phillip had been born a century or two earlier, he would have known greatness. He would have galloped his pony at full speed, alongside Crazy Horse, fighting to save our nation from the Bluecoats."

I smiled. "I can see him charging into battle, crying, *"Hoka hey!"* at the top of his lungs.

"Just like his great-grand uncle Crazy Horse," Grandma replied with a nod. "Phillip was a lot like Crazy Horse. He has that ancestral fire running through his blood."

I was suddenly curious. "How is it that you're not caught between the reservation and the outside world, like your sons are?"

"I know what world I belong to."

It was as simple as that. Victoria Chipps was the heart of the family. She stood her ground like a proud buffalo. Grandma's spirit was not restless, certainly not like that of Phillip.

I've come to understand that the reservation is a microcosm of life in the outer world. Traditionally, indigenous peoples are very concerned with the delicate balance in nature. Throughout all of life, there is always cause and effect, action and reaction. Whether we know it or not, we too are a part of that process to establish the subtle equilibrium that is necessary for life to thrive.

We spend our lives making thousands, millions of choices, and each decision we make, whether consciously or not, comes at a price. In choosing one thing, we say no to another. We are never sure of the long-term consequences of our selections. Rarely do we think of our choices as maintaining the balance of life.

What I learned was that among the Lakota, this knowledge is the basis of trading. It is a conscious attempt to maintain balance in nature and between all our relations. Knowing that there is always a cost establishes a conscious participation in the ever-evolving balance in the universe.

I thought of this that day, because I had not been fully clear on the agreement I entered into with the Chipps family when Phillip rescued me from underneath the trailer house and demanded that I walk. To me, it was as out of character as imaginable. Because of his drinking, you never knew when or if Phillip would show up at any given time. But when he was present, like the day he saved me, he was fully present. It took me a long time to truly consider the actions and counter-actions that took place that day.

That evening in the tent, I told Deodi about the conversation I'd had with Grandma, and by morning we had a plan: As we had done before, we drove Grandma the ninety miles to Rapid City for her favorite treat: a catfish dinner at Red Lobster, accompanied by those biscuits made with so much shortening they really did melt in our mouths.

Throughout the dinner we shared stories, laughing till we almost lost our food. Then we drove to the mall and walked around a department store to enjoy the colorful dresses and sweaters on the racks. Grandma had no need for much, but she loved to look.

As we walked the mall, I noticed as usual how the white people eyed Grandma suspiciously, looking at her clothing, her hair with harsh judgment. Although she made no sign, she must have noticed it too; nothing slipped past her. But for Deodi, who was half-Lakota with fair skin, and me, a white woman, it was obvious how separate, and yet how close, the Native and Anglo cultures were. We didn't let it upset us. As always, this small respite lifted Grandma's spirits. It was our special thing, our gift to her, and it made the two of us just as happy.

The rest of that summer, Phillip and I spoke, not regularly, but with more regularity than he spoke with the other Anglos in camp. He didn't seem to mind taking the time to answer questions I had regarding ceremonies. He not only told me how many offerings I needed, of which kind and color, and in what order, but he also took the time to share a deeper understanding of the rituals and origins of the ceremonies. He wanted me to have the correct information and to do the ceremonies in the right way. It was important to him.

I was going to the hill within two weeks of being pulled out from under the trailer house, and Phillip took an interest in that. In fact, it seemed that the whole Chipps family took an interest in my fast. Both Phillip and Charles helped me to prepare. Godfrey helped me to face my fears. Grandma was right by my side and gave me some of the sacred items I required. Grandpa nodded his approval the day we waited for the spotted eagles to descend from the clouds.

At last, everything was in place, including me. I was ready.

Chapter 12

The Fast

The morning of my fast dawned hotter and drier than usual, if such a thing were possible. I awoke with an odd emptiness in my stomach, as if I'd already started. Then it occurred to me: I had. As we prepared to meet the day, Deodi and I spoke little. Still I noticed she was extra gentle with me, as though I were about to undergo a serious operation. Then it occurred to me: I was.

Charles came around in his old Cruiser to tell me to gather my prayer ties, flags and sage, because we were going to prepare my fasting space. Charles told Deodi, a helper from camp named Susan, and me to get in the car. We drove as far as we could into the hills alongside the butte.

Cars are not meant to drive on the prairie like we did, but the old red Pontiac was used to a wild ride. I had to hold on tight so I wouldn't hit my head on the ceiling of the car when it plowed over the ruts and rises. I think my eyes were closed for more than half the ride. It made it easier to pray that the worn jalopy, and those of us inside, would arrive at our destination in one piece. The challenge was that the prairie grass was so tall that you couldn't see what you were about to drive over. Not that that fact made a bit of difference to Charles. The Lakota, and certainly the Chipps men, drove their cars hard, never adjusting speed, tearing across the prairie like they were riding wild ponies with their manes streaming in the wind. No one seemed to care about the chassis of the vehicle. Or the passengers inside, for that matter.

All at once, Charles stopped the car with a jolt. The prairie grass landscape had turned to rock. That meant it was time to get out and climb the remaining distance. It was a steep hike uphill, made all the harder by the precious cargo we carried. Every now and then we would rest to catch our breaths. On one of our breaks, Charles reached down and grabbed a plant.

He turned to us and said, "This is poison ivy. You should probably try to avoid it. It doesn't bother me. I'm friends with it." Then, he took the poison ivy and rubbed it up and down his arm.

Deodi, Susan, and I shared a grin. We were used to the Chipps family's immunity to snake bites, poison ivy, mosquitoes, and painful horse fly bites.

We had long tried to understand their relationship to nature and the elements. And for some reason, Charles found his tolerance to poison ivy a fact that bore repeating. Constantly. It had even gotten to the point at which we would roll our eyes and sing in unison, "We know, Charles. Poison Ivy can't harm you." It always lightened the mood, and it wouldn't have surprised me if he'd been in on the joke.

We trudged up the hill until we came to an area with relatively flat, grassy terrain, otherwise pretty indistinguishable from anywhere else.

"We're here," Charles said, in a calm, quiet voice. "Pick your fasting spot."

I looked around. Then I slowly circled the area, trying to get a feel for the land. After a few minutes, I found myself inexplicably drawn to a particular area. Once I was sure, I called the others.

"This is it," I said, trying, and failing, to tamp down my excitement.

Charles nodded his approval. "Okay. Let's prepare Oshada's *hocoka.*"

He began by cordoning off the area, marking it with prayer flags we set into the earth. Then he wrapped my prayer ties around each of the flags, making sure none of them touched the ground. He took the sage and laid it down inside the enclosure. Then he stood back a moment to inspect his work. I knew he was listening for any further instructions from the spirits, but they, and so he, seemed satisfied. Then he nodded again, and grunted.

"This is a good place," he said. "The spirits are happy. It's okay for you to come here. You'll be safe."

Charles took the remaining strand of ties and closed the "gate" on my fasting spot. Later, when we returned, he would open the gate for me to enter. I knew what would come next, of course. He would close it once again and leave.

Lumbering down the hill was much easier than making the ascent. Halfway down, we stopped for a rest. Once more, Charles reached for some poison ivy.

"Remember," he said with a frown, "Stay away from this. It doesn't bother me, but you probably don't get along with it like I do. It'll only give you trouble."

We were too tired this time to smile.

Once down the hill, we climbed back into the Pontiac. Now, Charles put the top down, which meant I had to hold on especially tight so I wouldn't bounce out of the car when it hit a deep rut. Despite our squeals—of both fear and delight—Charles seemed not the least bit concerned about the outrageous ride, especially now that the sacred items weren't traveling along with us.

When we returned to camp and, somewhat shakily, climbed out of the car, Charles pinned me with his coal black eyes.

"Have something light to eat," he said. "Then take a nap. I'll send someone for you when it's time for you to go." He left me to return to my tent. I knew where he was going. He had to speak to the fire tender about preparing the sweat lodge.

There was no turning back from this. Standing with my back to the tent, gazing out over the prairie, I felt that I was looking at my future. It was as bright as the South Dakota summer sun.

Later that afternoon, Charles sent a woman to walk with me over to the sweat lodge. To my immense relief, Grandma was there waiting for me. We shared a silent nod, then I loaded my pipe and set it on the altar. Grandma had made some special prayer ties for me, which she hung from the willow frame. Then, the two of us took a sweat together. There still wasn't any talking. It was as though we were beyond words. After a year of preparation, all that remained were the prayers. As Grandma sang them, I allowed any remaining anxiety and resistance to dissipate into the sacred sounds filling the air.

I saw fewer stones in the fire pit this time, but I had been prepared for that. I had been told that more weren't required, because the purpose of this lodge was different from most others I'd attended. The goal of this particular sweat was to create a separation between me and the world. The lodge became a doorway between two worlds, the ordinary and the supernatural. When I exited the lodge, I would be *wakan*, that is, holy or mysterious. I would belong to the spirits. And I would remain that way until I returned to the world through the lodge at the end of my fast.

While I sat in the lodge this time, I could feel the shift taking place. The lodge, the prayers, and the pipe were releasing me from my physical life and moving me into a spiritual dimension. The lodge was the portal through which I was changing vibrational fields, or worlds. I was being moved into the power in a very physical way. The shift was not due to a mental process, nor was it representational. It was physical in a way that felt utterly familiar. It was a form of mediumship.

When Grandma finished pouring water and praying, the flap opened for the final time. I emerged from the lodge backwards, behind Grandma. As I had been instructed, I looked at no one, and no one looked at me. The others faced away. with their eyes cast down to the ground. Grandma too looked down as she handed me my pipe and then wrapped me in my star quilt, covering my head so I could see no one even if I'd tried. She nudged my shoes at my toes, so I could slip them back on my feet. No one could see me or touch me directly, because the transition had occurred, I was wakan now. I belonged with the spirits. I no longer belonged with other humans. I was here in this world, but at the same time no longer in this world. My fate lay in the hands of those taking care of me, both the humans and the spirits.

Because I couldn't see, two women helpers walked alongside me, guiding my steps. They held onto folds of my blanket and gently moved me forward.

They put me in the front seat of Charles' car, and they got in the back. In total silence, we drove back to the spot alongside the bottom of the butte. This time, Charles drove cautiously. There were no bumps, and no need to hang on.

Once the car stopped, one of the women opened my door and gently helped me to my feet. Charles led the way up the butte to my fasting spot, with the women behind, helping to guide me. It was slow going. We had to make sure that not only did I not trip on my blanket, but, worse yet, drop my pipe. I had to trust completely and let myself be led one step at a time.

At one point, one of the women grabbed my covered elbow to keep me from stumbling. The other one steadied me from behind, putting her arm across my back. It was such a strange feeling, being wrapped in a spiritual blanket of protection, moving wherever and whenever I was steered. And through it all, there were no rest stops or idle talk of poison ivy. There was just the reverent, silent walk up the hill. No words had been exchanged.

When we arrived at my fasting spot, the women stepped aside while Charles pulled back the prayer ties and opened the gate to my hocoka. I slid off my shoes before he guided me inside. Then Charles closed the gate.

Just before leaving, he said, "I'm taking your shoes so you can't come down before your time. I'll bring them back when I come for you."

As strange as the day had been so far, I was a little stunned. It had never occurred to me that I would come down from the hill before the time I had pledged, but apparently, it happens. As I pondered this, Charles and the two women left.

When I was sure I was alone, I removed the blanket from over my head. I saw that the sun was fading into the horizon, and dusk was on the verge of settling over the butte. There we were, just me and the *cannupa wakan*, the sacred pipe. It was all I needed. I had prepared well. I felt secure inside my clearly defined rectangle of sacred space. I knew that my heart was sincere, and my prayers were strong.

By the time darkness fell, my eyes had accustomed themselves to the light of the moon, and I could see into the night. I felt safe and protected. Any remaining anxiety melted into the ethers and dissipated like thin wisps of smoke. There was nothing to fear. I was in balance with the land and the animals that lived on the butte. I was in right relationship with all my relatives, and I was protected by my prayers and the sacred pipe. In that moment, I completely understood the meaning of *hoka hey*. I was ready for whatever was to come.

I stood up with my pipe in my hands, and said, "*Hoka hey.*" It felt right. It was a good day to die and be reborn; that's what I had come to the butte to do. I was there to let go of the old and to embrace a new vision, a spirit-guided purpose for my life. I was there to surrender, just like I had done in the car accident, when I put my hands palms up in my lap and let go in complete trust. Just like I had done when I poured that last bottle of wine down the drain and said, "I won't drink anymore." And just like I had done under the trailer house after the storm, when Phillip commanded me to walk.

I thought about all the work I had done in my recovery, and how I had turned my life over to a power greater than myself. In that moment, standing barefoot on a bed of sage with a pipe cradled in my arms, I was doing what I had done when I chose a life of purification, without alcohol and drugs. And just like then, I had no idea how this surrender, in the presence of the grandfathers and the grandmothers under the starry sky of Creation, would affect the rest of my life. I could not imagine the life the spirits envisioned for me, or the deep satisfaction I would feel living the life they asked me to. I could not know with how many lives I would share my vision and this sacred connection. I had no idea how many addicts and alcoholics I would sponsor and lead to this same point of surrender. I could not grasp how many times in the thirty-five years waiting to be lived that I would pray the third step prayer with another suffering addict or alcoholic, with a dying or bereaved individual, or with someone who had lost their connection with the sacred.

Standing on my bed of sage, surrounded by strand after stand of the prayer ties I had made and holding my pipe, I prayed that third step prayer of Alcoholics Anonymous in my own words.

"*Tunkasila*, Grandfather, *Unci*, Grandmother, I offer myself to you. I am a pitiful two-legged, a woman, and I ask you to take pity on me and build with me and do with me as you see fit. Help me to let go of my selfishness and greed, so I can live the life you want for me. Take away my difficulties, so I can be an example for others, so they can see, through me, Your Power, Your Love, and Your way of life. Help me to keep my heart open, so I can walk on the good red road of the sacred pipe."

I knew of course that I would not be able to share with others the same physical surrender I was experiencing in that moment on Pine Ridge Reservation on top of Eagle's Nest Butte. Few, if any, would travel to a reservation and fast, as I was. However, the heart of the surrender would be the same. Anyone who has come to a point in their lives where absolute surrender is necessary understands that it takes heart to be brought to your knees. It takes heart to face your fears and admit your mistakes. To commit yourself to a new way of life.

That first night up on the hill, I deepened my commitment to *Wakan Tanka,* Great-Grandfather. In my head, I knew the language and the ways of the dominant culture, and in my heart, I knew the language and the sacred way of the pipe. Up on the hill, the pipe began speaking to me, helping me to understand how to fuse the two worlds.

I spent that night in and out of prayer, sitting, standing, and sometimes briefly falling asleep. The cold helped to keep me awake. Hunger and thirst were not an issue, at least not yet. I was being sustained by a force greater than food and water. In ceremony, such as I was, there is a vibrational nourishment that sustains the body and enriches the soul. The challenge is to maintain your commitment so as not to drop out of that elevated vibrational state. It is when you tip the scales more to the human end, rather than the spirit end, that hunger and thirst come roaring in. For now, I was able to maintain the balance I needed.

Day broke, and the morning sun was obscured by soft gray clouds. It was rare that the sun didn't scorch the prairie on Pine Ridge in August. August is the month for Sundance. It was always sunny in August. That day, however, the clouds were accompanied by a fine mist. It was a very good day to be up on the hill. I heard afterward that it had actually rained down below in camp, which was a good sign. Rain always brings nourishment.

My attention quickly moved from the weather to the pipe and my prayer ties. I was reminded that *hanbleceya*, fasting, was one of the ceremonies of the sacred pipe. The pipe sits on the altar listening to our prayers, waiting to be smoked. I thought about that, but more than that, I felt the meaning and lessons of the pipe in my heart.

How can I explain how the pipe came alive in my hands and spoke to me? All I can say is that my spiritual senses were in a heightened state of sensitivity. My clairvoyant sight opened, and I could see the purpose, the workings of the pipe. My clairaudient hearing opened, and I could hear the pipe speaking directly to me. My claircognizance, clear knowing, opened, and I understood the pipe from a profound place of personal knowing.

At one point my mind drifted, and I was reminded of the story of White Buffalo Calf Woman, Pte Ska Win, and how the pipe was brought to the Lakota people. The story came alive inside my consciousness. Memory of the story became a vivid reenactment of the pipe's being gifted to the people. There on that hill, I felt for the first time the power and presence, the deep inner meaning of the Calf Woman and her teachings.

Grandma had told me this story, and I could feel her praying for me. Grandma said, "Two warriors were hunting buffalo for food because the people were hungry, when out of the sky a cloud descended. From that cloud emerged a white buffalo, and it made its way toward the two men. As it approached, the white buffalo became a woman, a holy woman, and she was carrying a bundle.

"One of the men had bad thoughts about the woman, and a cloud of dust came over him. When it was gone, there was nothing left but a pile of bones where he had stood. The other warrior knew that the woman walking toward him was sacred. He dropped to his knees and bowed his head. Pte Ska Win told him to return to his people and tell them to prepare for her coming in four days' time.

"Four days later, a cloud appeared in the village, and a white buffalo calf appeared. As the buffalo calf got closer, she turned into the White Buffalo Calf Woman. She gave her bundle, which held the sacred pipe, to the people. She taught the people how to use the pipe to pray. She taught them the seven ceremonies that they were to perform to keep the Lakota Nation in balance. She told them that she would return one day to help them in the future. Pte Ska Win left the same way she had come, in a cloud that rose up to the sky.

In that moment, I was crying for a vision. I felt connected to life through the sacred pipe. I was inside the sacred pipe. The sacred pipe was inside of me. There was no separation. I have no idea how long I stayed inside the oneness I felt. By the time I opened my eyes, dusk had long since settled over the prairie.

Soon after, I felt a presence. I turned to find a buffalo standing beside me. I remembered when the buffalo came into the sweat lodge and stood next to me. Grandma was pouring, that is, running the lodge, in that sweat. I knew the buffalo was connected with her. I felt Grandma and Godfrey's pipe with me, and I felt at peace.

Next my attention was drawn back to my pipe that I had been cradling in my arms, as well as the prayer ties surrounding me. I thought about the prayers themselves. The prayers were enveloping me, protecting me, nourishing me. I understood that my life was connected to the spirit world through prayer, through my prayer ties, one for each of the animal nations.

When I say I understood, I mean that my understanding moved to a depth of knowing that goes beyond the connotation of what the word means. The understanding was one of reverence, devotion, connection. I understood that the prayers are the connection, but I had never *seen* the connection. Now, I saw the threads of energy between the prayer ties and the spirit world. I felt an overwhelming veneration for how the prayers represent the human spirit, my spirit, and the depth of the soul, my soul, reaching out to the guardians. I saw the prayers dance and come alive, and I was inside that vibration.

It was then that the bowl of the pipe moved into my heart. There was no difference between the catlinite, or red rock, bowl and my beating heart. I felt the stem in my body as well. The stem of the pipe merged with my spine, my spinal column, and my etheric channel. I felt my entire nervous system, controlled by the spinal column, infused with life.

I understood that the stem of the sacred pipe is the foundation of life. These weren't words that I was remembering from a teaching. I was experiencing this knowing firsthand. I felt the bowl sitting in my heart waiting to be smoked, waiting to be given away, waiting to have the joy of my prayers released into the world.

And then I heard the pipe speak to me.

"Life can be difficult. The spine can be broken, but the pipe, and the way of the pipe, helps to keep the spine strong. The pipe helps to keep the spiritual channel open and strong. The stem and the bowl of the pipe join together and work like one. The heart and the mind must join together and work like one. You cannot allow them to fight each other. They must work in unison in order to create happiness and goodness in life. The stem and the bowl of the pipe connect just like your neck connects your heart and your head. The point of connection, the neck, the throat, is where you give voice to the truth about all that you have lived, all that you dream, and all of who you are."

When I came out of my trance, I was surprised at how much time had passed. The sky was a rich indigo color. It was a vaulted canopy, bright with diamonds sparkling all around me. The stars were so close I felt like I could stretch my arms a little further and touch them, but instead, they were touching me. Slowly I became aware that not all the bright lights were stars; some of them were spirits. They were with me. The light of the moon was soft and pale in comparison to the bright lights I felt all around me.

I needed to pray aloud, and I needed to pray loudly. When I began to sing my prayers, I felt my voice being carried out to the universe. My heart and my mind were connected. The air coming out of my lungs, traveling up my throat, through my neck, to my open, singing mouth, was like the smoke of the pipe. All the prayers were released. I was giving all my prayers away and releasing my joy and gratitude into the world. I continued singing until the break of day.

At some point I began to see my prayer ties come alive with mystical power, Divine energy. The hundreds of prayer bundles all strung together became vibrant. Each one was aligned with a spirit. I could see that they were not "like" spirits, or simply offerings to a spirit; each prayer bundle was food for the spirits, and the spirits were alighting to take them. I felt blessed, and I remembered Grandma's insistence that I make all my prayer ties myself.

As dawn broke in the sky, I heard a voice.

"The ceremonies are the heart and soul of the nation, the Lakota Nation, my people. Without the ceremonies, the people will shrivel and die. The people are already dying. Alcohol and abuse have become a way of life. Babies are being born with their minds steeped in poison. Their thinking is soaked with the venom of alcohol. We had the courage to hope, but hope is being crushed out of those who are just beginning. The young ones are already committing suicide at a rate that that shames us all. We are losing the old ways. We are losing the ceremonies. It breaks my heart to see how everything is falling into ruin. It was not supposed to be this way."

I understood all too well what was being told to me. Although the same story was playing out everywhere, the Native peoples still living in the old way on reservations were like the miners' canary. I knew that they were the warning to the rest of us. They were sensitive to the changes in Mother Earth and felt her bellowing. In the ceremonies, they saw and felt her eruptions. There were many distractions in the world. It was becoming increasingly more difficult to feel the connection, one heart and one mind.

Sitting on my bed of sage, I breathed in the damp, almost minty richness of the plant, taking in all that I was feeling in those precious moments. I took a handful of sage and rolled it in my hands, put my hands up to my face and breathed in deeply. Then I rubbed the leaves on my face and arms and felt cleansed and awake. For quite some time I sat with my pipe, the spirits, and my thoughts. After two nights on the hill I was not tired, not anymore. I was charged by what I had seen and heard.

Eventually, I became aware of a presence that was dense, rather than ethereal. I saw Charles and Deodi emerge from the side of the butte. Both had huge smiles on their faces, and Charles was carrying my shoes. When he saw me he laughed and waved my shoes in the air.

It took me a few seconds to understand. I was done. It was over.

"I see you didn't need these!" he said. Then he gave me a once-over, scanning my spirit body and the light around me. With a satisfied nod, he added, "*Lela washte. Wopila, wopila.*" Very good. Great thanks, great thanks.

When I said nothing, he asked, "Are you ready to come out?"

I nodded and grinned, then let out a huge yawn. Charles pulled back the prayer ties at the opening of my sacred space. I came out and put on my shoes. Still cradling my pipe, I pulled my star quilt tightly around me. He gathered the empty strands of prayer ties and flags to bring back to the sweat lodge fire to be burned as a final offering.

We made a nearly silent trek down the hill and back to the car, with Deodi guiding me step-by-step by my elbow. She was right to be concerned for my balance, because after all those hours in one place, I needed to regain the hang of walking. I could feel the love pouring out of her to me, and I felt Charles simply bursting with pride. But I couldn't hug either of them until I came fully back to the world through the sweat lodge, which is where they were taking me.

On the way down the butte, Charles saw a patch of poison ivy. Unable to miss the opportunity, he picked up a handful of leaves and said, "Remember, leave this alone. It's not a problem for me, but it could cause you trouble."

The fast would not be complete until I went into the sweat lodge and was fully released from the spirit world back to my human life. Grandma was there waiting for me. The stones came in one by one, and, as always, the first five were honored for the four directions, as well as the marriage of heaven and earth. Grandma called for a few more and began to pour the water. The heat rising from the stones soothed me. It warmed me from the inside out. I breathed in deeply, taking the steam, the cedar, and the sage into my lungs till I could feel the life pour back into me.

Grandma and I both prayed our wopila, the thanksgiving prayer for my fast and for being returned safely to life. Some of the prayers were sung, and others spoken. Then, as is the custom, I described to Grandma everything that had happened while I was on the hill. Charles sat outside the lodge, so he too could hear what I had to say.

After I finished speaking, I withdrew from the lodge, and Charles took my pipe inside the ceremony house. Later that night, Godfrey conducted a five-stick ceremony for the purpose of gaining knowledge. In that ceremony, he went to the spirits to speak to them on my behalf, and they in turn relayed my vision and everything that happened while I was up on the hill.

The spirits told Godfrey what they had said to me and showed me during my fast. They told him how much I was able to see, hear, and feel, because I might not have been aware of it all. Or I might not have remembered, or not been able to take in all that occurred while I was with them. The five-stick spirits told Godfrey if I fell asleep or was able to stay awake and pray the entire time. Then we smoked my pipe, and the ceremony was over.

Afterward, depending on what the spirits allowed Godfrey to tell me, he interpreted the parts of my vision that I did not understand, or perhaps couldn't remember. Depending on what the five-stick spirits told Godfrey, he might disclose that I would have a dream in a year, or five years, that would clarify something I was given. He might suggest that I come back to the hill within a certain time frame, or that I was done for now.

Finally, Godfrey would tell me what parts of my vision were real, were actually the spirits, and which parts I made up—that were my subconscious or delusional thoughts I wanted to believe. It is easy to deceive ourselves in the matters of visions and messages from the spirit world. Sometimes, we want to believe something so badly that we cannot distinguish our own thoughts from what we receive. It is important to work with a teacher who can help clarify the difference.

After the five-stick ceremony that night, Godfrey left the ceremony house and waited for me to come out. Bursting with excitement I asked, "What did they tell you?"

I knew right away I had made a mistake. The question should have been, "What can you tell me?"

"*To*," he said, with a curt nod. The word, pronounced "doe," roughly translates as "good." Not like *lela washte*, which means "very good," as in something you are excited about. *To* is a cross between "yes," and "good," kind of like "yup."

"Do I need to go back to the hill anytime soon?" I asked.

He shook his head. "You're done for now."

I saw that I would have to wait for my vision to unfold. But it didn't really matter. I felt a tremendous sense of peace. I understood Godfrey's nod. I intuitively knew the unsaid words that lined up behind his "To." The Lakota way is one of action, not words.

Shortly after my fast, Godfrey came to me and said, "Oshada, you're going to pour tonight. Make sure to put your pipe on the altar." I considered it quite an honor to lead the women's sweat lodge, but he had made the pronouncement with the same fanfare as when one would say, "Hey, while you're at the store pick up some milk. Don't forget to put gas in the truck."

I quickly came to understand that pouring wasn't so much an honor as increased responsibility. I learned that these so-called promotions were about service to the pipe. Now, if I made mistakes, they would come back on me and on those I loved. I had to pay attention, and above all else, be honorable rather than honored.

Chapter 13

After the Fast

After my fast, life settled back into a routine. The people kept coming out to the Chipps camp for healing, and the ceremonies were still taking place. There was a never-ending flow of those who were suffering and in pain. Each one who came had a pressing need, and no one was ever turned away.

I never tired of the near-nightly healing ceremonies. I felt compassion for each of the souls who had made the journey to South Dakota, and I felt gratitude for my own good health and the opportunity to be of service. The way of the ceremonies is a life of service to which Grandpa, Grandma, Charles, Phillip, and Godfrey had dedicated their lives. Those of us in camp who were following the way of the pipe became helpers. Our lives, too, were dedicated to the Yuwipi and the spirits, and we did whatever we could to ensure the smooth running of the ceremonies.

By this time, I had long since surmounted the difficulties that I had encountered when I first came to the Chipps camp. I showed my commitment to the ceremonies, and, as a result, I went from being tested to being trusted. I was still an outsider, of course, and as such I felt honored and enormously grateful to have been able to learn about the ceremonies and the Lakota spirits on a deeper level.

In time I came to appreciate the great joy, as well as the great responsibility, of the Yuwipi ceremonies. Most of the lessons that I learned had to do with restoring balance within the individual, and within the world. Those who made their way out to the camp and were successfully doctored by Godfrey's Yuwipi spirits had done something in their lives to earn the blessing that was being given to them. Not everyone gets a second chance. Very few people have the opportunity to have direct spirit intervention in their lives.

There is a difference between having knowledge, something that you know in your head, and, knowing it in your bones, having an abiding wisdom that comes from self-sacrifice and personal experience. With age and experience comes a deeper sense of meaning, as well as compassion. I began to see the stream of sick people who came through the Chipps camp as part of the human condition, a condition that I was not separate from. Having worked in a healing capacity myself, I knew that physical disease was a soul sickness. Pain and suffering are a dis-ease of the soul. This is a lesson we all have to face at different times in our lives.

The real illness that Godfrey and his Yuwipi spirits were curing was the illness that clouded the soul of each person who put up a healing ceremony. Different personalities and equally diverse genetic make-up resulted in the manifestation of physical illness in correspondingly distinctive ways. It wasn't limited to the individual, but to their environment, as well. The healings always had to do with creating balance within the individual and Mother Earth.

It always came back to balance. Every exhausted and anguished patient who came out to the reservation was desperate for help. Each one had to surrender, give up the control they thought they had. Each one was presented a mirror in which their own life was reflected back to them, and they rarely liked what they saw. If they were willing to face the parts of themselves that they previously had not wanted to look at, they received the opportunity of a lifetime.

The cold weather and an early snow closed down the ceremony house on the Chipps land, just like Grandma said it would. Godfrey and the family took time to rest, but after a while, the family went out on the road. Godfrey loved to travel. He and other family members mostly visited the New England area. Godfrey was building a following there, and he always had invitations to do sweat lodges and healings.

Meanwhile, Deodi and I left camp and went home to Massachusetts, where we often joined the Chipps family on whatever farm or homestead they were staying. Everywhere Godfrey went, there were always forlorn parents with a desperately sick child, or someone with a serious diagnosis. Sometimes for five or six nights in a row there would be sweat lodges and Yuwipi ceremonies.

Results varied depending on how strong the ceremonies were. It was difficult to maintain the level of energy and commitment that was needed night after night. People came pledging many things. Often, there were more promises of sincerity than there was actual follow-through. It was a tough lesson for Godfrey to learn. He was still living with a foot in the world he grew up in and knew, and a foot in a foreign world with an unfamiliar culture. Mistakes were bound to be made. As a result, Godfrey suffered, and, his family suffered.

There was rarely a straight line between cause and effect, however. When mistakes were made, future deaths and tragedies were attributed to those mistakes. We heard stories of men who disrespected the ceremonies only to die mysteriously within the following year. In Western culture, we might view this as superstitious or coincidental. I came to see that the ritual was an exacting process by which the consciousness had to be properly prepared. The ritual set the consciousness, and if there was disrespect, or a mistake, this set the wrong frequency, resulting in a boomerang effect.

In the world view of a medicine family, everything that happens in life can be traced back to the ceremonies and the medicine man's altar. Tragedies happen in all families, but in the Chipps family, misfortunes were generally tracked back to a spiritual cause or violation. The accidental or sudden death of a child or grandchild in the family was generally seen as a result of the desecration of sacred protocols. I personally knew two different men, from two different decades, who were responsible for setting up Godfrey's altar for a period of time. Both of these men lost a child in tragic circumstances, possibly because of ceremonial mistakes.

The stakes are high in the healing ceremonies, and the specific requirements for each ceremony are what create the portal to the spirit dimensions. Yuwipi medicine is a precise practice just as medical surgeries are.

Here's how I look at it: Generations of Lakota Yuwipi men rarely, if ever, left the reservation. They worked curing Native ailments, illnesses that were part of the prairie, the buttes, and the deprivation that a Yuwipi man and his spirits knew. They understood the etiology of these diseases. The influx of outsiders with diseases not previously seen on the reservation, or in the traditional healing ceremonies, was a challenge. Even for Godfrey. So precision was very important.

I watched Godfrey's powers increase with age, dedication and regular fasts. There are levels of Yuwipi men, and at each level there is an increase in powers to cure illness, as well as in responsibilities. Whenever Godfrey completed a fast, he was given the vision and the increased powers he needed to continue his work.

In my stay on the Chipps land, I discovered a vision pit dug by lineage ancestors. The pit is like a large grave, dug ten feet down into Mother Earth, with steps carved out of earth into a side wall. Godfrey, family members, and extended family fast there in the summer months. The pit is covered with branches that span across the opening. Once the person is inside the pit, the branches are covered with tarps that block out daylight. There are no distractions in the pit. There are no clouds to stare at, no starry nights to marvel at, or playful winds to warm or cool the body. Godfrey went to the pit regularly to maintain his powers and to commune with the spirits. It was where he learned what was needed to maintain balance between the Earth World and the Sky World, between the humans and the spirits.

Chapter 14

The Way Back

After we returned home to Massachusetts, Deodi and I continued to expand our understanding of the Lakota ceremonies. We also worked in our own shamanic healing and mediumship practice, which we named Lost and Found after the lyrics of the hymn "Amazing Grace" that talks about being lost and blind and then being found and able to see. We had both been wretched and in the throes of addiction. We had been lost and blind to the reality all around us. Finally, Grace found Deodi. Then, Grace found me. An amazing, undeserved Grace had given us both a second chance.

We decided from the beginning that the promise of Lost and Found was not to heal clients, but to help them find themselves. We have all lost something on this journey called life. We've misplaced our self-esteem, our courage, or our hope. Some of us have lost our dignity, the ability to practice self-love, or the capacity to trust. Deodi and I helped people look at what they'd lost and the process by which they'd lost it. Then, we worked with them to find and reclaim those parts of themselves that they wanted back. It was deeply satisfying work.

Then, in February, with the holidays over and the deepest part of winter upon us, the phone rang. It was Grandma, telling me that Phillip had been in a terrible car accident. At first, the family had little information regarding his condition, but it was eventually determined that his spine had been damaged, and he lost the use of his legs. He would never regain his ability to walk and left the hospital in a wheelchair. For the remaining five years of his life, there he remained. Reservation life is a challenge and it takes a toll on everyone. It co-exists side-by-side with the sacred and the ceremonial.

The news was not unexpected, but it was horrifying nonetheless. We knew that car accidents and liquor were an integral part of Native life, that the extreme poverty and disenfranchisement lead to a profound hopelessness that co-exists with the sacred and the ceremonial way of life. We knew that the young on Pine Ridge, certainly in Wamblee, have low expectations of what life will have to offer them when they grow up, that many do not even know there is a life beyond the dusty roads that crisscross their reservation lands. These losses of life, limb and opportunities are not just felt by the injured one. They are felt by everyone. After all, we are all related, *Mitakuye Oyassin*. Now, Deodi and I felt them, too.

As soon as we could the following spring, we returned to the reservation. As before, the ceremonies continued in spite of all the setbacks. The desperation that filtered down to the children was the most devastating to witness. I saw an entire generation of babies struggle with fetal alcohol syndrome and fetal alcohol affects. You could see it in their vacant eyes and their inability to develop language skills. Grandma would balance her grandchildren on her hip as she walked and tried to soothe them. She did her best, but she could not stop their teenage parents from drinking, nor could she stop the devastating effects on the children who cried. Learning disabilities and cognitive deficiencies would plague these children for the rest of their lives.

There was little I could do. As I have said, my years of sobriety didn't translate to the lives of the people with whom I was living. My experience came from a world alien to theirs. An outsider could never understand the deep tentacles of poverty and the severe genetic disposition to alcoholism. The help and the outreach had to come from within the culture, and there were those who worked tirelessly to instill pride and a sense of self-worth in the younger generations.

There were Lakota who got sober and could speak the language of recovery to their people. They translated their encouragement into a meaningful cultural context. The Chipps family needed the ceremonies to define their lives as much as the people needed the ceremonies to relieve them of their suffering.

Soon it was time to go home, back to the reservation. Actually, Deodi and I didn't just visit this time. We had decided to move to South Dakota. It wasn't quite a well-planned decision, but it wasn't out of the blue, either. We wanted to return, but on our own terms. We rented a house in a small town adjacent to the reservation, called Kadoka. It was a stopover for bikers who made their annual pilgrimage to Sturgis for the end of summer bike rally.

Our house was next to a local church. When we first moved in, we heard soft baby cries on the second floor. We made some inquiries, only to find out that our rental used to be the local hospital, and the maternity ward had been upstairs. For some reason unknown to anyone, the sounds still echoed throughout the old house. Sometimes, Deodi would go upstairs and sing lullabies to the crying babies. The singing seemed to help, because eventually the crying stopped.

There wasn't much to the town. Kadoka's biggest attractions were the truck stop off I-90, the large animal veterinary clinic, and the dinosaur park tourist attraction, which happened to be owned by our landlord. Otherwise there was a post office, an insurance agent, a couple of mini-marts, and a coin-operated laundromat where, in the summer, the bikers stopped to do their laundry.

The rule of thumb in Kadoka was that you didn't lock your doors. If you planned to be away for an extended period of time, you locked the front but not the back door, in case a neighbor needed to come in to borrow something or deal with a burst pipe. Around town, especially in the winter when it was freezing, you also left your car running while you popped into the post office or to buy some groceries. After all, there wasn't any sense in getting back into a cold car. And if you needed help moving something heavy, you called the coach from the high school, and he sent over a couple of boys from the wrestling team to help you out. In other words, it was real small-town living.

When we left the East, we had sold all our furniture, because it was cheaper to buy new, mass-produced furniture rather than ship ours across the country. Among our neighbors, we were considered fancy to have new, store-bought furniture with matching lamps. Most of the prefab, government issued homes in the area didn't have much in the way of furniture. Furniture was a luxury.

An outstanding feature of the interior of our new home was very old, very ugly wall-to-wall shag carpeting. We asked the owner if we could replace the carpeting at our expense. There was a discount place nearby, and we could afford it.

The landlord hesitated. Finally he said, "Well, um, when you all leave, that shag carpeting won't lay back down like it is now, nice and flat. It doesn't work so good once you take it up and then try to put it back down. It curls up in the corners."

I looked at him in disbelief. "But we're going to get rid of the carpeting and leave the newly installed carpet for you!"

I'm not sure that he believed me, but he let us go ahead.

Both townies and Native friends scratched their heads at our extravagance. After pulling up the shag carpeting, we rolled it to the edge of the lawn and affixed a sign to it that read, FREE CARPET. PLEASE TAKE ME.

Half an hour later, a man knocked at the door, apologized for his intrusion and said, "Ma'am, are you sure about that carpet? It's all right for me to just take it? Are you sure you can't use it for something?"

When we assured him that it was his, he was obviously thrilled about his good fortune. He was going to use it down in his basement and couldn't thank me enough.

It was experiences like this that helped us truly understand how necessary the community and its medicine men were to the Lakota people. Neither the government that had displaced them, the ranchers that convinced them to lease their lands, nor the missionaries that cut their hair and punished their children for speaking their native tongue were going to help these people. They had to rely on each other.

Deodi and I quickly settled into our new house. Despite its quirks, we were well aware that we were living in grand style compared to the government-issued homes in Wamblee. Not only did we have tables, chairs, and sofas, we had hope. We had choice and the freedom to come and go. There were only the two of us. We were not three or four families, couples and their children, living under one roof.

We continued to participate in Godfrey's Yuwipi meetings, and even after all this time, I never ceased to be amazed by them. Each ceremony was both the same as the others and yet very different, as well.

There was a young man who came the following summer who had been diagnosed with AIDS. At the time, before the development of effective treatment, there was rampant fear about HIV and AIDS. AIDS was considered a death sentence. Nonetheless, John arrived in camp one day after having met Godfrey earlier that year at a healing gathering out east. John arrived wanting to put up a ceremony, but his weakened immune response made it difficult for him to survive the living conditions in camp.

I helped as much as I could. Late in the day before his ceremony, John, with limited energy and little dexterity, had spent countless hours painstakingly assembling his bundle of four hundred and five prayer ties. Then, an unexpected ceremony needed to be held, and John was asked if his prayer ties could be used. He knew there was no way he could say no, but he panicked at the thought of making another four hundred and five tobacco offerings for the next night.

Grandma, who had asked for his ties herself, told him not to worry. But John was a worrier, frantic that he wouldn't be able to have his healing the next night. He needn't have bothered. Early on the afternoon of John's ceremony, Grandma and I set to work, making the hundreds of bundles required, with plenty of time to spare. John was both grateful and amazed, not only that we would do that for him, but that we had finished so quickly.

Later that night, after the sweat lodges, we went to the ceremony house for John's Yuwipi. It took a little while to bring in the bucket with the stones so we could steam everything being used in the ceremony. Finally, close to midnight, the altar was set up, and it was nearly time to start. Before the Yuwipi could begin, however, there were two people who wanted to make flesh offerings for John's healing.

A flesh offering is serious business. When you think about it, the only thing that we truly own in this life is our bodies. Everything else, all our loved ones and all our possessions, even our memories, are gifts that we are given, and that can be taken away. So when we want to make a deep sacrifice, we give a part of ourselves to the spirits by giving them a part of our bodies.

Those participating in the Yuwipi meeting can give flesh offerings for their own ceremonies, or on behalf of another. Before the ceremony begins, people go to the *hocoka,* the sacred space, and tell the Yuwipi man or his assistant how many flesh offerings they want to give. A sharp knife, which has been steamed but not sterilized, is then used to cut small pieces of flesh from the person's upper arm. These pieces of flesh are wrapped in a prayer bundle, or sometimes put inside the Yuwipi rattles.

As soon as the flesh offerings were made, Godfrey put his hands behind his back, and two men tied his hands and fingers with a bowstring. Then they put the star quilt over Godfrey's head and body, and wrapped him like a babe in swaddling cloth. As I had seen before, they bound him in it with rope. When the binding was completed, the two men stood on either side of Godfrey, who leaned forward into their arms, trusting them completely. They gently caught him, picked him up, and laid him face down on the bed of sage.

Now we were ready to begin the Yuwipi ceremony for John. The door was sealed, and the one small light was turned off. The altar, the prayers, and the singing were all strong that night. John's anxiety brought his vulnerability to the surface, and he was able to pray from his heart. We all did the same. The spirits quickly appeared, and Godfrey's rattles lifted off his altar and flew around the room, touching several people before moving to John.

The singing reached a fever pitch, as did the spirit power. Spirit lights flashed around the room, sending white and sometimes blue sparks flickering onto the ceiling, the walls, and right in front of my face. Once the power was in, I could sing the songs and devote my entire being to singing. Loud noises, thumps and stomping, bounced around the room and outside the perimeter of the building. It was like being in the eye of a thunderstorm. The spirits were happy, and the power was palpable. There was no mistaking it.

The rattles and the spirits moving them gathered around John, who sat up front among Godfrey's helpers. One of the men told John to stand, in order to make his prayers even stronger. As he did so, John started to pray out loud, and the dancing rattles touched him on his head, arms and entire body. They thumped on his chest and back, and up and down his legs for quite some time. John cried his prayers to the spirits, making himself pitiful so the spirits would be merciful to him. I couldn't hear his prayers with all the singing and loud noises, but I could certainly feel them.

How to describe what it feels like to be inside the womb of the ceremony house when the power is strong, and the spirits are filling the empty space with palpable life? In the light of day, the wooden shack standing on a dusty patch of land in the middle open prairie that is the ceremony house looks as though it would collapse under a strong huff and puff. But once the drumming and the prayers begin, the ceremony house becomes a spiritual vessel or container. While sitting in the ceremony that evening, Godfrey's altar came alive with power and communally transported us into a different dimension of time, or rather non-time, and space. We were on the threshold of the spirit plane, no longer in ordinary reality. Or rather, we were taken to the edge of human consciousness.

That night, the spirits explained it to me directly.

"The Yuwipi man is brought into the spirit dimension covered and bound, so he cannot see or hear except that which we wish to make known to him. You in the ceremony are waiting to receive him back into your world. When he is with us, he is floating on a moving plane, plates of consciousness that exist between the worlds.

"The cooperation between human and spirit in a legitimate Yuwipi meeting is a sacred experience," they told me. *"It is not just the medicine man that enters into this non-ordinary reality. The spiritual interpreter, the Yuwipi man, enters more fully into the spirit world having gone through the portal; however, the participants are also allowed to witness and partake in this mystical interlude, where time and space are suspended between the worlds."*

Once the spirits doctored John with the rattles, the ceremony was complete. The spirits untied Godfrey, and, as always, they threw his star quilt at someone sitting up against the wall who had been praying and singing. Then a candle was lit, and Godfrey sat cross-legged in the middle of his sage bed. The pipe was smoked, and we all offered prayers of thanksgiving.

Afterward, it was time for the feast. A helper passed out paper plates and plastic spoons and forks, along with the simple food. Soon the room filled with laughter. Then the same helper prepared a spirit plate, with a small portion of all the food at the feast, for the ancestors. The fire tender left the ceremony house to take the offering plate to the Chipps family burial plot and leave it for their relatives in the spirit world. This was a way of giving nourishment back to those who came before, and in whose medicine lineage we were walking.

It was just before dawn before we emerged from the ceremony house that night, bleary-eyed and exhausted. As always, the healing took a lot from Godfrey, and he was fast asleep before the last of us left. It would be a couple of days before Godfrey would be ready for another Yuwipi ceremony. To my understanding, this was the first time he doctored someone with AIDS. It was a huge undertaking. AIDS was not a traditional Indian sickness. This was a new level of medicine for Godfrey.

John, on the other hand, was revitalized. He said he felt more energetic than he could remember having been in a very long time. He stayed with us in camp for another week before heading home. As the months went by, he called in reports to Grandma on how he was doing. His diagnosis from a full-blown case of AIDS diminished to a diagnosis of HIV. After about six months, the doctors told John that apparently there had been a mistake, that he had been misdiagnosed. His viral load was insignificant, and there was no longer cause for alarm.

A year later, John returned to the reservation to do a thanksgiving ceremony, a wopila, for the spirits. One morning, about five a.m., there was frantic knocking at our front door. A gasping, breathless John, with all the blood drained from his face, started rambling in short, nonsensical sentences. We saw at once that he was in the midst of a full-fledged panic attack. Deodi and I managed to calm him down until he was able to speak coherently.

"You know Raymond, Godfrey's cousin? Well, he has a gun. He's drunk, bad drunk. He's threatening to kill Godfrey, and Janis. He's not making any sense. He started shooting! And Godfrey had to get the gun away from him. I ran out of there. I can't go back. I don't know what I'm going to do."

John had never faced a madman waving a pistol and making incoherent threats, let alone been caught in a crossfire. That was more reality than he was prepared to tackle. He spent the morning with us before packing his belongings and leaving the reservation. Mercifully, no one had been hurt, and the gun disappeared back into the shadows, where it belonged.

I was in touch with John off and on over a period of several years, and he continued to thrive. But he never returned to the reservation. I can't say I was surprised, or that I blame him. Although we continued to participate in ceremonies, that shooting was the beginning of the end for our Lakota experience, as well.

Chapter 15

Sorrow

That summer, like all other summers on the reservation, there were many who came for healing ceremonies and to be put out on the hill for fasts. Phillip still came by, but it was difficult for him to maneuver himself and his chair around the camp. The newcomers mostly left him alone. Those of us who knew him approached with caution. If you had any questions about the preparations for a particular ceremony, he would answer, but he had changed. His drinking grew along with his bitterness, although I did manage to have an occasional meaningful conversation with him from time to time.

While Phillip struggled to remain whole, it was clear that he was no longer the man he used to be. Godfrey, meanwhile, was broken-hearted over his brother's misfortune. Any time he could, he employed the spirits to doctor Phillip, but there was only so much they could do. Ironically, perhaps, Phillip's fate could not be reversed. Sometimes, we are on a one-way street on our journey.

I have come to understand that others, even loved ones, are often powerless to do anything but bear witness to the decline of those they love. It is a devastating process, but we do come into a fuller relationship with the sacredness of life, as well as our own humanity. We learn to walk with death and our own vulnerabilities. We can rail against it and become bitter, or, we can make peace with misfortune and death, and vow to be of service. As always, it is our choice.

In the meantime, Ellis Chipps had Alzheimer's and was fading into a shapeless void that bore little resemblance to the strong and powerful Yuwipi world he once know. Grandpa's life was coming to an end, and again, there was nothing that could be done. Like the prairie grasses that blow in the wind, otherworldly winds were blowing through Ellis Chipps—and more and more of him was being carried away to the spirit side of life.

There was nothing that could be done for either Phillip or Grandpa Ellis except prayer and making them as comfortable as possible, so we did both. One night, after a sweat lodge, Grandma asked if someone would stay in the lodge all night and pray for her husband. She was too old and worn to spend the night there herself. When I volunteered, Grandma kissed my forehead and thanked me. She was distraught at the thought of losing her husband.

After Grandma left the lodge and the others left the area, she closed the flap, kissed her fingers and patted the willow frame with a final, lingering blessing.

It was a quiet night, and the remaining heat of the stones kept me warm. I saw no flashing spirit lights, spirit animals, or visions. Instead, I simply prayed for an old man who had served his family and the spirits well over the course of a lifetime. I prayed that the spirits would be kind to him when it was time for them to come for him. The pipe and the sweat lodge were a fitting tribute for a man who lived by the pipe, who had given so much of his life so that the people could live.

I knew that for the Lakota, it is never about the individual lives. It is always about the Lakota people, the *Oglala Oyate*. Medicine lineages continue on generation after generation, so that the people can live. The medicine trickles through the land and the people. It wends its way like the water that moves through the rivulets it carves into the earth. The people are an everlasting stream of individuals that merge into the Lakota Nation.

After that night, Grandpa made several trips to and from the hospital in Rapid City but to no avail. He died in April, 1990. There was a great outpouring of feeling from the community, and he was mourned in the traditional way. In traditional societies grief is externalized. It is raw and immediate, pulled to the surface so that the bereaved can feel its sting and move through it with the support of the community.

After her husband's death, Grandma took a pair of scissors and cut off her braids. There was no ceremony or vanity to her actions. She simply grabbed one braid, then the other, and cut them off. Her short hair was a sign of mourning. Everyone who saw her knew that her husband had died.

Then she and her sons took Grandpa's few articles of clothing and personal items and burned them in a fifty-gallon oil drum. Burning his personal effects pushed the ones left behind to let go even more. The letting go is intense, bringing death's wound to the surface in order to provide the momentum for those left behind to deal with the reality of the loss.

Grandma left the countryside and went to Wanblee for a while. As her female relatives and community members came to visit her, their grief covered her like a blanket. With every meeting, the other woman and Grandma fell into each other's arms, keening loudly. The visitor cried even more loudly than Grandma, to override and shield her anguished sobs, so that no one could hear her profound vulnerability.

Ellis was buried on the family land in the basin of Eagle's Nest Butte. After the extended wake and funeral, Grandma returned to the Chipps camp out in the country. As her hair grew back, her grief subsided. A year later, she was able to braid her hair once again into her trademark double braids.

Our years in South Dakota faded one into another, full of remarkable healings, extraordinary visions and, most of all, a depth of love between this world and that of the spirits that imprinted a legacy on my soul.

I had long known that there is a delicate balance between the worlds. A relationship to the spirit world is available to each of us, depending on how much we are willing to invest in our spiritual lives. Moving between the worlds requires a level of attunement to which not many people are willing to dedicate themselves. It is not about technique or tricks; it is about love and compassion.

My life was intimately united with the sacred, and I knew that I was Divinely protected in mysterious ways. The Lakota say, "*Taku Wakan*," which refers to all things mysterious, and, "*Skan*," the motion of the universe. All things in the universe move in mysterious, or hidden ways inside the Great Mystery. I've come to accept that perhaps the greater part of life is unseen, secreted inside our consciousness waiting for us to discover it.

When I first began this healing journey, I had survived a car crash that could have easily killed me. I know the only reason I survived in one piece was because of an inexplicable voice, which may have come from a vast wellspring of inner knowing, or from the cosmos. I survived after having been pinned beneath a ton of galvanized steel. My body was left intact inside the handlebars of a fallen motorcycle. For years, I had heard the sounds of invisible spirit motorcycles whip around the outside of the ceremony house during healings. I cannot help but think that it was these same spirits that wanted me to live.

These experiences and the knowledge they brought meant the world to Deodi and me. However, life in the Chipps camp was becoming more polarized and dangerous by the day. The sacred and the profane had always lived side-by-side on this land, but now, the gulf that had separated the two was being obliterated. Lines were becoming confused and violated. It became increasingly more difficult to rationalize staying. Michael's words reverberated in my head: "Stay as long as you can. Stay unless or until your lives are in danger."

One November day during this time, we heard that Michael Harner and Sandy Ingerman were offering an advanced course on death and dying that had not been a part of our training program. The class was focused on journeying to the land of the dead in a shamanic state of consciousness. We would learn how to assist souls crossing over from this earthly life to the next.

This was a different approach from mediumistic communication. Spiritualism is about the light, so there is no peril in communicating with the so-called dead if you are trained as a medium. But because shamanism deals with the light and the dark, there is always a risk. However, with the Core shamanism Michael had developed, there was no altar, which made an enormous difference. Both the stakes and the results were mitigated.

Deodi and I were invited to the training, so we decided to make the trip to Denver, where it was being held. We looked forward to spending time with Michael and Sandy, whom we hadn't seen in over a year. Plus, we needed a rest after the long season of ceremonies. The first snow of the season had already come to Pine Ridge, so there would be no more ceremonies in camp for a while.

We were looking at about a four hundred-mile drive, and we took our time. We drove about halfway the first day and stopped for the night at a motel. The next day, we drove through Denver. We were on I-70, headed to the higher elevations of the Colorado Rockies. The temperature was in the low forties, and a light drizzle was misting the windshield. We could hear the slosh of the wipers as they squeaked, clicked, and spread the trickle of water across our view of the growing fog. As we climbed higher, the temperature dropped ten degrees. The rain turned to slush, to hail, to snow. Deodi turned the heat up to eighty-five, and the defroster to full speed to fight the condensation on the windows. The asphalt was greasy, and every time the tires rotated on the sleet-coated road, I could feel them slide and catch again.

Deodi was from Maine and knew how to handle a car in winter conditions. I was usually confident in her driving, but this time, I was anxious. I could feel her focus and the tension in her body as she gripped the steering wheel. I stared straight ahead, clutching the arm rest. My legs were taut. I could tell I was scared, because my right foot kept jumping to hit an imaginary brake on the floorboards in front of me.

No sooner did Deodi bark, "Stop that! It's not helping!" then we hit a patch of snow-covered black ice. The tires spun, and we were launched airborne into sheer, towering, unforgiving rock.

I mentally reviewed Driving School 101, searching for the page that said turn into the spin, or turn out of the spin. Which way did you turn? For Deodi, it was pure instinct. She was no stranger to negotiating black ice. When she felt all hope was lost, she said calmly, "We're going. Pray."

So I prayed. The 1989 Buick Riviera slammed head-on into a wall of solid granite. Neither of us had buckled our seat belts after the gas stop in Denver. I closed my eyes and surrendered myself into the deep quiet of prayer while the car jack-knifed, rolled over and landed upside down in a ravine.

In that moment, in that prayer, in that surrender, I felt the soft paw pads of an enormous bear embrace me. I flew through the air, metal crushing, squealing, and disintegrating, and I bounced around inside warm, fleshy pads of a giant grizzly. His claws were retracted, and all I felt was the cushioning of his plump mitts.

The seconds passed. I lay face down on the ceiling of the overturned car. My lower legs and feet stuck out of the shattered passenger side window. I backed out of the window, inch by inch, on my belly, sliding my belly and hips over Deodi's shoulders. Once out of the car, I pulled myself up on all fours and waited for my head to stop spinning. Deodi was now in the passenger seat, where I had been a few minutes before. The driver's side on the vehicle was completely flattened. If she had been wearing her seat belt she would be dead, crushed. She was still pinned, her breath was shallow, her pants torn, legs red and swollen.

Time slipped away in the moments during and after the crash. We were both in shock, not quite sure what world we were living in. Then the state troopers arrived and called the ambulance. The black ice was creating havoc for everyone, and cars continued to slip and slide off the road. Most of them glided into a ditch at the base of the mountain.

The rescue team that came had to slide a board into the vehicle and strap Deodi to it, to pull her out from the passenger seat. Once we were safely out of our car, we settled into the back of the trooper's Jeep. We helped guide him as he towed vehicles out of the gully and back on the road.

Eventually, an ambulance arrived and we climbed into the back. Two female Native American EMTs took our vitals and looked us over. I appeared to be fine, but they wanted to take Deodi to the hospital to be checked further. The inside of her leg and knee were red and swollen from hitting the console when she was thrown into the passenger seat

Deodi spoke to the EMTs in Lakota. They stopped what they were doing, came over, sat down, and we all prayed together. We remained silent for a few minutes, until the energy field shifted. A healing power enveloped us all.

When we finished praying, the head EMT paused and said, "*Lela washte*, it's all good. You can go. Take care now." Both women nodded as we left the ambulance. There were other injured people who needed their help far more than we did.

By that time, the wrecker was on scene. He loaded our totaled vehicle onto the bed of his tow truck. Meanwhile, he told us to get in the cab and stay warm.

"I don't want you girls catching a cold on top of everything else you been through today," he said.

We stepped up into his cab and made ourselves comfortable on the worn leather seat, with Deodi in the middle. There was something about the dog-eared seats and the smell of pine freshener from the scented Christmas tree hanging from the rear-view mirror that made me feel safe. I wasn't aware of having held my breath, but now I felt like I could breathe again.

The trucker climbed up, took off his hat, and said, "I'm Mike, and I'm gonna take real good care of you girls. I don't want you to worry about a thing."

Deodi's teeth were practically chattering with the cold, so he proceeded to turn on the heat full blast. He looked at her, lowered his voice and murmured, "Don't you worry, little lady. You're gonna be okay."

She turned to me, tears in her eyes, and whispered, "He looks just like Pepe."

Pepe was her mother's father, who was on the spirit side of life. The resemblance was so striking that she couldn't help staring at him. As for me, Mike reminded me of Jack, the man who took care of me when I was pinned in my car fourteen years ago. He had the same reassuring manner.

Whoever Mike resembled, we both got the strong sense that he was an angel sent from above. He simply could not do enough for us. His presence was so reassuring that we completely relaxed. Still, he wanted to make sure we were both warm enough.

"You girls might wanna take your gloves off," he said. "Why don't you rub your hands and fingers to get the circulation going real good? Then, put 'em up to the vent and feel that nice hot air. Make sure your feet are nice and dry, too. You can take your boots off if you want."

We did as we were told. It felt so good not to have to make any decisions.

"I'm gonna take you down the mountain to a small town with a real nice motel," he continued. "You might want to stay there a night or two till you get situated with the insurance company. When you're ready, call me. I'll get you set up with a rental car."

Then he let out a long breath. "I'm towing your car right down the street from where I'll drop you. The insurance man, Al, will know where to find me."

He shook his head. "You sure were lucky. That black ice is real tricky, even if you know what you're doing." Then he proceeded to tell us how someone else had a rollover crash in the same location we did.

"They weren't as lucky as you girls. One of 'em . . . well, never mind. The important thing is that you girls are okay. Yup, you're gonna be just fine."

As we drove down the mountain, Mike told us to look over to the right. There was a kind of service road, adjacent to I-70, that rose onto a little hill. A sign read, "Truck Ramp."

"Sometimes the trucks lose control when they're comin' down the mountain. Their brakes don't kick in, especially if it's a little bit slippery. The driver can turn up one of those run-away ramps, and it'll slow him down so he can get control of his rig. Once they stop, they can back down and get on their way."

He nodded and fell silent for a bit, and I sensed that he was remembering something that had happened there. Sure enough, after a while, he said, "It usually works pretty good, except once last year, things didn't turn out too good. There was a guy hauling horses. He had about a dozen in there. He couldn't get control of that truck and slow it down enough. He got to the end of that run-away ramp, and he was still goin.' That was real sad. His truck and all those horses. . . . "

At this point he stopped talking. What he had told us sunk in, and an ominous silence filled the cab. Finally, he said, "Yup, it was real sad."

The shock and sorrow, and the realization of our good fortune hung in the air. No one spoke the rest of the way down the mountain.

As promised, Mike dropped us off in town at a little motel. He nodded to the clerk at reception.

"Take real good care of these girls," he said, slapping a giant hand on the counter for emphasis. "I just brought 'em down from up near Golden with that mess they got goin' on up there. I'm gonna take their car over to the shop, so they'll be here a few days."

The insurance office was just a few doors down, he told us, and if we felt up to it, we could go over the next day. He would tell the agent where we were and what had happened. Once again, he assured us not to worry about anything and that we would be okay. In the meantime, we had a clean, warm room, and we were safe.

Deodi and I were both black and blue, and very sore. She iced her leg off and on, till the red turned purple, and the swelling subsided. Before long, she was able to flex her knee and walk on her leg with the help of a cane. We rested for three nights at the little hotel before leaving.

We had a lot of time to think during those few days. We talked about how there are several portals through which we can leave this earthly life, with no penalty attached. In other words, for whatever reason, our souls have completed their mission and are free to leave the physical body to return home to the spirit world. We have fulfilled the karma that we agreed to complete when our souls entered into human expression.

The soul, after all, has an intelligence far beyond our mortal understanding. On a much deeper level, or, if you will, on a far greater plane of understanding than we consciously grasp, we choose the where and when of our death. In the crash, we could have left our physical bodies behind, but for some reason not clear to me then, neither of us chose to. Instead, once again, we were saved by the spirits who loved us. My soul was not ready to slip away, and neither was Deodi's.

Needless to say, we did not make it to the shamanic training on death and dying. But we did experience several shamanic journeys in an effort to make sense of the rollover, and to figure out what to do next. We were both still in shock, which interfered with the clarity we needed as we looked for answers.

At one point, I turned to Deodi and asked, "Do you think we should call the Chipps family to tell them what happened?"

She pursed her lips. "I'm not ready. I'm just too scared right now. What if we're under attack from the spirits? What if we made some mistake in the ceremonies?"

"None of it makes sense," I said. "Here we had this horrible accident in which one or both of us could have been killed or paralyzed, and yet we were protected from harm. You know as well as I do that those hands that held us as we flew through the air were real. Obviously not the same kind of real as you find in ordinary reality. But from the moment the car took off, those hands were as real, as present, as any human hand I've ever held. I will never forget them."

She shook her head. "Me neither."

The insurance company worked out all the details, our bruises were healing, and it was time to drive back home to South Dakota The car was a total loss, so we returned to Kadoka in a rental. We arrived home safely, and although Kadoka was a welcome sight, we were somehow both feeling skittish.

The next day, we felt ready to drive into Wanblee and tell Grandma and Godfrey what happened. Grandma put her arms around both of us and shook her head. She wouldn't let go, and when she finally did, tears ran down her cheeks.

Then Grandma mumbled a prayer in Lakota. When she finished, she reached for me, held my face between her hands, and said, "I'm so glad you're okay. I can't believe this happened."

She turned to Deodi and did the same. When she was done, she seemed both relieved and angry. She spoke a few clipped words to Godfrey in Lakota that neither of us understood. But we could tell by her tone that something was going on.

In a soft voice, Godfrey said, "You're going to be okay. Everything will be all right." Compassion filled the air when he spoke this way. I was deeply touched, and I believed him.

We found out later that Charles was upset that we hadn't called him from the scene. Charles loved long-distance driving and insisted that he would have driven through the night to come pick us up and bring us home.

In spite of the warm welcome, however, we were starting to second guess ourselves, as well as everyone else.

Chapter 16

In Conclusion

We no longer had a home out East to go to, but we didn't want to spend the winter in Kadoka, either. We both knew we needed both distance from the reservation and perspective.

"Deodi," I said one morning after a particularly restless night. "Why don't we go to Florida?" She looked at me in surprise. "Think about it. We can get a small rental near my parents' apartment."

She nodded slowly. "Not a bad idea. It wouldn't hurt to be close to family and friends. I'm not ready to return to all that upheaval in the Chipps camp."

We remained in contact with the Chipps family by telephone. We knew that that first winter without Grandpa would be a hard one, and Grandma and her sons could not get past their grief. Grandma urged us to come home as soon as the soft winds started to blow across the prairie in the springtime.

We understood. She needed everybody to be together. She needed to rely on others for strength, and she needed people who understood what was necessary to keep the ceremonies going. Grandma knew that Godfrey would require all the support he could get with his father gone from this world, not to mention Phillip in a wheelchair, still struggling to cope with his new reality.

Slowly, Deodi and I allowed the horrible memory of the crash to fade into the background. After all, we'd been protected. There wasn't any reason to think that such a thing would happen again. At least that's what we told ourselves. Still, we were reluctant to return to Kadoka and the Chipps camp in the spring.

Then I thought of the expression, "In for a penny, in for a pound." Neither of us wanted to put an end to this precious time, this gift we had been given years before. Leaving what we had started, in spite of the danger we'd survived, was simply unacceptable. It had made good sense to leave South Dakota for the winter, but in the springtime, we needed to return to the reservation and the ceremonies.

On the surface, everything went back to the usual routine of life in the Chipps camp: the families, the individuals, the needs, the hopes, the preparations, ceremonies. The pipe had become my life. The ceremonies, the healings, the spirit power were also my life. I did not want to leave this way of life, but I kept thinking of Grandma's words when we first arrived. "One day you will have to leave."

By now we both understood that our life on Pine Ridge with the Chipps family was temporary. At some point, we were supposed to return to the dominant culture and bring the heart of what we had learned to the people. It was becoming clear that time was coming.

That summer took a toll on everyone. Tensions grew high. Deodi and I were now living a life that was spiraling out of control. There were more accidents and injuries, not for us, but for others out in camp. Disagreements could not be explained or justified. Drinking, drug use, and acting out among the brothers and other relatives escalated. The ceremonies were still taking place, but the necessary balance and harmony weren't there.

Nevertheless, I was not prepared for the day that Grandma came to both of us and said, "You have to go. It's time for you to leave. If you stay any longer, you will be too deep inside the ceremonies, and you won't be able to leave. You know how it works. You know what will happen. The pull will be too strong."

She looked out over the butte. "Your life isn't here. It's in the outside world. Teach others how to live in right relation to themselves and the pipe. Go. Be a bridge."

We understood. Grandma acknowledged the violence and petty jealousies, but she had to stand by her boys. Still, she didn't want anything bad to happen to the two of us. She wanted us to be safe. She wanted us to be the living pipe and carry that understanding to the outside world.

As it turned out, we stayed in Kadoka another year, but we spent time in another camp on the Rosebud reservation. By the time we left, it was a bittersweet end to the years of living separate from the dominant culture and in a sacred manner deeply embedded in ceremonial life.

Over the years I lived on the reservation, I devoted myself to the ceremonies of the sacred pipe. It's not so much that I believed in the pipe; I knew it. I trusted it. There is a great difference between faith and knowing. When a person has faith, they believe some unknowable truth is real. They use their faith to bridge the gap between doubt and belief. When someone knows something, it is because they have experienced it in the depths of their soul. They do not require faith. What they know may be what some consider an unknowable truth, yet they know it.

I came not only to know the power of the pipe and its ceremonies, but also to know the love and compassion of the spirits. I knew when I left the reservation that I was supposed to be a link between the Lakota way of ceremonial life and the spiritually starving, dominant culture. I knew I was also supposed to be a channel, to the best of my ability, between humanity and the spirit world.

I thought back to what I knew of my recovery work. In AA, we have a saying: "We may be the only version of the Big Book of AA that someone will ever know." In other words, after years of studying the principles of AA, of doing our work and becoming whole, we incorporate the program to such a degree that we become it. We are a living, breathing Big Book, and we can show by way of a living example the healing we have received. When this shift occurs, it is common for others to say things like, "There's something about you; you seem so peaceful." Or, "It just feels good when I am around you. Maybe you can help me."

I found the same to be true of the ceremonies of the sacred pipe. I needed to incorporate the pipe and its ceremonies into my way of being in the world, my very presence in the world. I had to be a living example of what I knew to those in the outside world. Incorporating the ceremonies of the sacred pipe was all about cooperation between the worlds. I had been given an opportunity to witness and know the heart of the ceremonies. I was charged with bringing the heart of the ceremonies to those in the dominant culture because few would have the opportunity to live what I had been privileged to experience.

I learned from my immersion in Lakota culture that there is power in an eagle feather or fan because of the relationship the person who carries it has with the spirit world. The feather becomes alive only in the hands of one who is united in spirit with the Eagle People. It is not the other way around.

Sacrifice earmarks our sincerity. All we truly possess is our bodies, and we give them to make ourselves pitiful and demonstrate our sincerity. The medicine men and women who have a historical and spiritual birthright to the Eagle People and eagle feathers have sacrificed: flesh has been offered in ceremonies, serious pledges have been made, they have danced in the Sundance arbor—sometimes with eagle feathers sewn into their flesh, and then had them torn from their bodies as an offering.

The eagle does not empower us; we must do the work to secure the connection. Once we have sacrificed and made the connection to the Eagle People, they will work through us, lending us their power. If our connection is really strong, we can sweep our hand over an ailing body and the power of the feathers will flow from our fingertips.

The power moves through us; it is not inherent in the fan, nor in us. The fan is an extension of the power to which we are attuned. The fan is an extension of our hand. Our hand is an extension of our heart. Our heart is an extension of our spirit. Our spirit, our spiritual essence, is an extension of *Wakan Tanka*, who breathes life into us.

Deodi and I left Pine Ridge and the Rosebud reservations for the last time in 1993, six months after Phillip died in yet another car crash. We lived in Florida for several years, and then moved to Westford, Massachusetts. During those years, we continued our healing work, shamanic practices, and mediumship devotion with clients and students. The learning and teaching never stopped. I found a satisfying outlet with my original love, Spiritualism, and became a certified medium, commissioned healer, and Ordained Spiritualist Minister.

Grandma remained the matriarch of the Chipps family until her own death in 2009, at the age of ninety-one. I will always remember her as an unstinting teacher who was happy to share her knowledge. She knew just whom to share what with, and when. She had an impeccable sense of timing, and was an extraordinary judge of character, which was important, because at the Chipps camp there were daily tests of sincerity.

Grandma's eyes always told what she was thinking or feeling. She could flash you a look that said, "Not now," or "Pay attention." My favorite look was the twinkle in her eyes when she was deferring her power to another, or letting someone learn a lesson on their own. That same twinkle could show up when the flap was about to close on one of the door openings in the lodge. You knew it was going to be a hot one when her eyes lit up and she started the round by saying, "*Hoka hey*."

Then, sadly, Deodi died in 2014—probably not coincidentally, within three months of Godfrey and also Charles. As I grieved them all, I continued bridging the gap between the material world and the spiritual world. I continued to serve the Spiritualist churches and my clients. My understanding of the relationship between the spirit world and humankind continues to deepen. In my work, I do not simply relay messages between the worlds. My goal is to reunite souls that have been separated by death. I want my clients on both sides of the veil to feel like they have had a visit. I see this as a healing mission that serves those on both sides. Both the incarnate and the discarnate souls need healing and a meaningful understanding that life and death are two sides of the same life.

It is also a part of my ministry to be present for those who are preparing to leave this material world and make their journey to the spirit side of life. Alleviating the fear of death and being fully present in the face of it is an honor and a privilege. Over the last several years, I have devoted myself to yet a deeper understanding of, and relationship with, the spirit world through trance work.

Meanwhile, as I look back at my years with the Chipps family, my relationship with Phillip remains the most enigmatic. Since living on Pine Ridge, my connection with him continues to evolve. How could I not wonder about Phillip's resolve that I walk, only for him to lose the use of his own legs? Was this a coincidence? A predictable consequence of alcohol and driving? Or, was it a trade of sorts? I don't know, but I cannot help but think about our connection. I have come to believe that Phillip and I made a covenant a very long time ago, probably long before we both came to the earth plane in this life span. The roots of our soul contract extend beyond any conscious recognition.

Not far from our home in Westford, Massachusetts, was a street called Phillip Drive. Whenever I drove to the main road, I saw the green signage with Phillip's name in bold, white letters. Every time, my thoughts went to Phillip. I never thought of that street name as a mere coincidence. It was a constant reminder of Phillip's presence and the bond we shared.

In 2019, I sold the house in Massachusetts and moved to Florida. I left many things behind when I made the move. I said my goodbyes to parts of my life I thought were over. The day I left Massachusetts, I drove by Phillip Drive one last time and said goodbye to my old friend. I believed that Phillip and I were finally parting ways.

Moving was a huge undertaking. After arriving in Florida, it took the better part of a year just to settle into this new chapter of my life. Then, after about a year, I had a dream. That day, it had occurred to me that virtually all my teachers had moved on to the spirit side of life. I was the last one standing, the only one left to tell our story. But what story was I to tell, and how to tell it?

This dream, really a profound visitation, has remained with me ever since. I was on Pine Ridge out in the Chipps camp, standing behind a car and getting ready to open the trunk. It was the kind of day you relish and try to hold onto, a beautiful spring afternoon with azure, cloudless skies, and prairie grasses swaying in the breeze. I had stopped to look at the sky and enjoy the warm sun on my skin when I felt a presence and turned my head. That's when I saw Phillip walking toward me.

When he stopped alongside me, I gave him a warm smile and said, "Phillip, you look good. It's wonderful to see you."

I was so glad to see him happy and in his prime, seemingly in the best of health. He looked dashing in a crisp shirt, tucked neatly into stylish slacks.

After a brief greeting, he looked at me closely and said, "*The family saved you for a reason.*"

Then he evaporated as quickly as he had appeared. I woke immediately from the dream state and relived it over and over again. I recorded it and listened to it dozens of time, going over every detail with a fine-tooth comb in my mind. I understood exactly what it meant, even though in all those years, it had never occurred to me that the Chipps family saved me from under the trailer house for a reason.

One month after having the dream conversation with Phillip, at the promptings of my dear friend and mentor, Colin Bates, I started writing about my experiences in Spiritualism and ceremonial life. It was then that I realized what Phillip was saying to me. He, and his family, wanted me to write this book, to write about them and their medicine lineage as I had experienced it. It never occurred to me back then that the time and teachings they invested in me were part of their vision for the future.

The Chipps family extended their vision, the vision of their grandfathers, to future generations, to each one who has taken the time to read this story. Each of us is a part of their legacy, as well as that of Crazy Horse and Woptura. Each of us is a part of the spiritual legacy of all the great teachers and holy people who have walked this road of life before us. Their teachings, their love of the spirit world, as well as the compassion of the spirit world, move through each one of us. It is our obligation and our blessing to keep it alive.

I have been a Spiritualist for more than forty years. That path has been interrupted with many detours. Each one of the detours brought an even greater depth of understanding to my work with the spirits, and their work with me. I have loved working in Spiritualist churches, presenting lectures and platform work, as well as private readings. In the course of this career, I did not envision ending up on not one, but three different Native American reservations, one of which would become my home for many years.

I have come to understand that we are all in a process of excavating and remembering. We all have the capacity to know the fullness of who we truly are, not just the ordinary reality of what we see, feel, hear, taste and smell. Many of us believe that we are a body with a soul. Some of us recognize however, that we are a soul, first and foremost, with a body. My journey on the earth plane, just like everyone else's, is to remember my soul's purpose.

Adapting to the physical world is our common challenge. Sometimes, we need to clear away enough of the debris and heal the scars we carry to remember why we are here on the earth plane. Just as we all have a unique set of finger prints and DNA sequencing, we also have an irreplaceable spiritual imprint, our etheric body. Our spiritual bodies are our spiritual DNA.

Speaking of DNA, it's important to bear in mind that no two of us are alike, either physically or spiritually. We are one-of-a-kind people and one-of-a-kind spirit. It is our responsibility to understand and respect the exceptional gifts that each of us brings to creation. Our physical lives and our physical gifts are obvious, and if we wish, we can choose to live on a purely physical basis. However, if we are ready and able to access our own Divinity, we are not only saving ourselves, we are also saving humanity.

Like a true Scorpio, I have faced death and walked with it unscathed. Death didn't want me yet. Close as I've come to it, I've never had a near death experience, wherein I left my body and was offered the opportunity to go to the other side of life. I have, however, been warned, guided, and protected from death. I do not consider myself invincible. My soul is simply not ready to leave the earth plane. Clearly, there is a plan in place, and undoubtedly, I still have work to do. Or, perhaps, I am simply a slow learner who has not learned the lessons at hand.

As I have said, I have related this saga, as well as the context that made it possible, only because I have been asked to do so by the Chipps family. My years on Pine Ridge is not a casual story and is not to be taken lightly. I have held this part of my life very close to my heart. I have entrusted these memories to very few.

My purpose here has not been to document all the healings and cures I have witnessed, but rather to open readers' minds to the unexplained possibilities in the universe. Some people may believe that such healings are feasible; others may not. But I have seen a world of human and spiritual potential that most of us have not known to exist, much less tapped into. And I have felt compelled to share it.

I am relatively certain that for many, what I have written in these pages is neither reasonable nor conceivable. You are not alone. I admit that there is a lot of room for duplicity and outright fakes. However, there are many studies that speak to the legitimacy of such phenomena, as well.

There are many books and articles on the subject. I have witnessed posers who claim to be doing things that are not authentic. As a Spiritualist minister, teacher and respected medium, I have wasted no time in exposing such individuals. In most cases, these characters assumed no one would know better, that no one had seen the true phenomena. They relied on the vulnerability and even desperation of those seeking proof that their loved ones lived on.

The people I speak about in this book may have been the subjects of controversy, but, in my informed opinion, they are the real deal. Controversy and skepticism go hand-in-hand with that which is extraordinary. That is why many such gifted mediums, shamans, and medicine people keep a low profile. They demonstrate to small, private groups. They are not seeking fame.

My relationship with the spirits developed like any friendship. First you trust, and then you trust a little more. The only difference is that my guides did not disappoint me like another human had the power to do. Instead, they persevered. They were steady. They always had my best interests at heart.

My years on the Pine Ridge and Rosebud reservations led me to the deepest and most profound part of my life. They are the most soulful part of my journey, and the memories take me back to a place where my heart feels at home. Those years were bursting with a history that fills me with both a reverence and a sorrow, both of which are unfathomable, truly bottomless.

It was a privilege and a calling to live there; both a fortunate and a dangerous calling. Fates that I consider worse than death were potentially part of
the tradeoff.

I moved to Pine Ridge, and then to Kadoka, wide-eyed and innocent. I
believe that what saved me was my sincerity. The spirits have loved me for
my unwavering dedication. They have stood by me, they have always stood
by me, because they know my heart. The spirits are my heart.

Epilogue

There is a place within each of us, a great and sacred point of stillness between the in-breath and the out-breath. It a place where Wakan Tanka *resides within our souls. It is a place we are each capable of touching, a place we are all capable of knowing. Inside that sacred space we can feel the whole of the universe. Here we understand what it means to be sacred, to be close to the Great Mystery. Here we understand what it is to be in the moment, not achieving, not doing, simply being, being in the eternal moment.*

For what is it that we really want to achieve with our lives? What is it that we are all striving for? What is it that we all want to become, except to achieve oneness, connection? We need to connect with our own spirit. We need to connect with Wakan Tanka*, the Great Mystery. Without it, we are nothing.* Wakan Tanka Kici Un. *May the Great Spirit walk with you.*

—My Lakota Spirit Guide

In 2015, months after Deodi graduated to the spirit side of life, I had a reading with a British medium, Bev Mann. She was visiting the First Spiritualist Church of Salem, in Salem, Massachusetts. I am closely associated with that church and have served their congregation for the better part of thirty years. I arranged to have a reading with Bev and asked the church president not to give her any information about me other than a first name. I was an Ordained Spiritualist Minister but did not want her to know that, nor that I was a medium.

When I met with Bev, she brought me delightful proof of continued life regarding my partner and the love of my life. Deodi had a dry wit and was outspoken in this life. Nothing changed on the other side. It was wonderful to receive proof of her unceasing existence and to experience that personality does indeed survive the change called death.

After several touching messages, Bev declared that Deodi was a vegetarian, which I affirmed. Then, she said my partner was speaking about a butcher. Bev paused and we were both a little puzzled. Then, with a chagrined look on her face, Bev declared, "She's making fun of me for eating meat! She's quite cheeky, isn't she?"

That was absolute proof of continued life for me. Who else but my partner would take a jab at the medium that was bringing her through for the first time? Deodi's ease at communication and her sense of humor told me more than anything that she had indeed survived death.

Deodi had communicated all that she wished to convey to me, but we still had a few minutes left in the reading. At that point, Bev said she did not know why, but she wanted to give me a picture that she had carried around in her purse for years. She took out the picture and handed it to me. I immediately recognized it as Gordon Higginson.

Bev was quite taken aback. She had never physically met him, but felt close to him. I said I knew him and had worked with him. I told her it did not surprise me that he had a hand in the reading. When Deodi and I were at Stansted Hall in the mid-eighties, Gordon took quite a liking to her. He had a deep affinity to Native American guides and culture and knew about her Native heritage. He even invited Deodi and me to accompany him on a trip to Wales.

It made perfect sense that Gordon Higginson was there to greet my partner when she crossed over to the spirit side of life. It made perfect sense that he was right by her side to help her with her first communication. Deodi was an excellent medium while on the earth plane, but now that she was in spirit, she would have to learn how to communicate through a medium, and not receive communication as a medium. Gordon made his presence known in the reading and let me know that he was looking out for his friend, and me.

This brought me a tremendous sense of comfort, of actual joy. I had not felt joy since the death of my beloved partner. As a medium, I understand that there is no such thing as death, and that life continues after the change called death. However, when we lose someone who is dear to us, who is in our inner circle, our hearts are broken. It takes time to heal the shock to the physical body and our emotional well-being.

Knowing, having evidence from an outside source, that my much-loved partner was still very much alive, albeit in another dimension was deeply gratifying. It was not the same as being able to hold hands with her, feel her presence on the other side of the bed, or enjoy a meal together, but the reading brought the two realities together as one for me. Mediumship bridged the gap between the worlds on a deeply personal level, and it made an enormous difference in my grief process. In fact, it made all the difference.

Wakan Tanka Kici Un.
May the Great Spirit walk with you.
May the grandfathers bless you.

Afterword

Sal Gencarelle

Oshada Jagodzinski's book is a deep dive into a unique journey of developing a profound and personal relationship to spirit. What is offered here is more than just an individual account of a life dedicated to spirit, but also nuggets of universal wisdom that the reader can easily access and learn.

Like Oshada, I also lived for extended periods of time on the Pine Ridge Indian Reservation in South Dakota and learned from the Chipps Lineage. Reading the stories of her time on the reservation as she immersed herself in the spiritual practices of the Lakota Sioux people brought back many memories. I can verify her testimony and understandings are valid and real—and her telling of her experiences accurate and true.

The journey Oshada describes is not one that many people get to take, and even fewer people are able to share with the world. She reached out to me early in her writing of this book and explained how the ancestors came to her, informing her that her life was saved for bigger purposes than she understood at the time. She felt the pull to share her story through writing a book but was hesitant. She had my empathy, for sharing such personal encounters is not easy and comes with many challenges. But, I said, "If the ancestors are telling you to share your story, what choice do you have?"

I'm so proud and happy that she has written *My Life Among the Spirits* and is willing to share with you this incredible tale. This is not just a fascinating story, but also teachings of wisdom, spiritual connection, and deep truths that can change your life and bring you closer to spirit.

* * *

Sal Gencarelle is the founder of Director Helpers Mentoring Society.

About the Author

Oshada Jagodzinski is an ordained Spiritualist minister and certified medium in Boca Raton, Florida. Since 1979, she has worked internationally as a medium, lecturer, teacher and shamanic and energy practitioner, having trained extensively in the U.S. and Europe with some of the most distinguished experts in the field, including Gordon Higginson, medium and president of the Spiritualists' National Union, for twenty-three years; Michael Harner, shaman and cultural anthropologist; Twylah Nitsch, lineage holder of the Seneca Wolf Clan Teaching Lodge, and the Chipps Lakota medicine family. Oshada combines shamanic healing practices and both Western and Eastern energy healing modalities in her practice, called Lost and Found. She trains mediums, holds spiritual development classes, and works with the bereaved, as well as with those preparing to transition from this world. She does readings and consulting and can be reached through her website at www .oshada.com.